COVER ILLUSTRATION: From left to right (in chronological order) are the flags of the Texas Revolution. First is the Mexican tricolor emblazoned "1824" signifying support of the federalist Mexican Constitution of 1824 which SantaAnna set aside. Next is the "Come and Take It" flag flown by volunteers refusing to surrender their small cannon to Mexican forces at the battle of Gonzales, October 1835. Third from the left is the "Bloody Arm" flag displayed at the La Bahia presidio, Goliad, in December 1835. Next is the two-star tricolor that briefly flew over the Alamo as Santa Anna's army approached in February 1836. The two stars represent the Mexican states of Coahuila and Tejas/Texas. Last is the single-star first official flag of the Republic of Texas, December 1836.

The Texas Revolution
Tejano Heroes

COLONEL ROY F. SULLIVAN, USA (RET)

authorHOUSE®

AuthorHouse™
1663 Liberty Drive
Bloomington, IN 47403
www.authorhouse.com
Phone: 1-800-839-8640

First published by AuthorHouse   12/09/2011

ISBN: 978-1-4685-2341-6 (sc)
ISBN: 978-1-4685-2340-9 (ebk)

Printed in the United States of America

CONTENTS

Roy F. Sullivan, Colonel, USA (Ret)

OTHER WORKS BY ROY F. SULLIVAN:

"Scattered Graves: The Civil War Campaigns of Confederate Brigadier General and Cherokee Chief Stand Watie"
"The Civil War in Texas and the Southwest"
"Escape from Phnom Penh"
"The Texas Navies"
"Escape from the Pentagon"

OVERVIEW

"In the seven months struggle, that began as a war to prevent Santa Anna from destroying the federal system and after seven months changed into a movement for independence, the Texas Mexicans were represented in every aspect of the conflict. Some were supporters of the centralists and fought with Santa Anna's army to suppress the Texas revolt. Many joined the Federal (Texas) Army and participated in the siege and attack on Bexar, while a few served in the hastily organized governmental bodies like the General Council that undertook to give some direction to the revolution. Others were a part of Dimmitt's and Fannin's commands at Goliad and a small group died with Travis at the Alamo. In some instances the Tejano contribution to the Texas cause was not appreciated by some of the Anglo-Texans, and in a few cases they were maligned and accorded unfair treatment. Despite these provocations, part of the Tejanos championed independence and risked their lives and futures fighting to make it a reality."

(George O. Coalson, "*Texas Mexicans in the Texas Revolution*")

AUTHOR'S NOTE

Certainly I have erred in overlooking many Tejanos and Tejanas who bravely and resolutely contributed to the Texas revolution. I also apologize for misspelled or incomplete names. Records—such as military rosters—were not always maintained during the revolutionary period. Misspellings, even among extant records, were common. An example is the "Angel of Goliad" whose last name was probably Alavez or Alvarez but could have been Alavesco, Alevesco or Alavesque.

CHRONOLOGY OF SELECTED MAJOR EVENTS

1681. The first permanent settlements in Tejas are established on the Rio Grande River near El Paso, Texas. These missions are Yselta del Sur and Socorro del Sur.

1690. The Mission San Francisco de los Tejas is founded near present day city of Weches, Houston County, Texas.

1700 Mission San Juan Bautista is relocated to a site on the south side of the Rio Grande River near the city of Eagle Pass, Maverick County, Texas.

1746. The Spanish crown selects Jose de Escandon to begin a systematic colonization of Tejas. An example of a land recipient was Tomas Sanchez who received a grant on the Rio Grande River in 1755 on which present day Laredo, Webb County, Texas was founded.

1801. Don Martin de Leon y Galvan arrives in Tejas with his family. Five years later he establishes a large ranch on the banks of the Aransas River. He began petitioning the Spanish governor in San Antonio for more land but his requests were denied. Subsequently he moves his family near present day San Patricio, San Patricio County, Texas.

April 1813. In San Antonio Bernardo Gutierrez de Lara issues a Declaration of Independence from Spain. It is the first independence proclamation for Tejas. "We are free and independent and have the right to the establishment of our own government."

August 1813. Spanish royalist forces defeat Tejas republican troops at a battle at the Medina River, the bloodiest battle ever to take place in Tejas/Texas. Commended after this battle, in which some 1,000 republican troops were killed, was a royalist lieutenant named Antonio Lopez de Santa Anna. This first Tejas revolution ended with Santa Anna and other royalist officers publicly executing every tenth republican prisoner in the military plaza of San Antonio. Jose Antonio Navarro, a supporter of the revolution against Spain and a future signer of the Texas Declaration of Independence from Mexico, escapes and spends three years exile in Louisiana. Fighting at the Medina and escaping with Navarro is his uncle, Jose Francisco Ruiz, also a signer of the Texas Declaration of Independence March 3, 1836.

December 1829. Moses Austin, father of Stephen F., petitions the Spanish government to allow him to bring American colonists to Tejas. Governor Antonio Maria Martinez in San Antonio recommends approval and forwards Moses Austin's petition.

July 1821. Stephen F. Austin arrives in Tejas to assume the colonizing responsibilities of his deceased father, Moses. Stephen is greatly assisted and advised by Tejanos Erasmo Seguin and J.M.J. Veramendi of San Antonio.

August 1821. After a protracted struggle the Spanish government recognizes the independence of Mexico.

April 1824. The Mexican government grants the petition of Martin de Leon y Galvan to settle forty-one families from the Mexican State of Tamaulipas on lands between the Guadalupe and Lavaca rivers in Tejas. De Leon was the only Tejano empresario to receive such authorization.

October 1824. The Mexican Constitution of 1824, a federalist, liberal document, is signed, becoming the law of the United Mexican States. The first signature on the Constitution is that of Lorenzo de Zavala.

December 1826. Benjamin Edwards, brother of empresario Hayden Edwards, organizes thirty dissatisfied settlers in Nacogdoches to revolt against Mexican authority during the short-lived Fredonian rebellion. The uprising lasts only six weeks and is put down by Mexican militia, part of which is commanded by another empresario, Stephen F. Austin. The militia arrives in January 1827 to find the conspirators gone and the rebellion ended.

March 1827. The constitution of the Mexican State of Coahuila y Tejas is adopted.

April 1830. The Mexican government issues its law of April 6 banning further immigration from the United States, including the importation of slaves. The government also establishes customs houses and troop garrisons to enforce this unpopular decree at several Tejas coastal ports of entry.

June 1832. Lieutenant Colonel John (Juan) Davis Bradburn arrests Francisco Madero, William B. Travis and others for violations of the Law of 1830. Bradburn, of Virginia and Kentucky, is a mercenary serving in the Mexican army. Previously he had closed all Tejas ports except Anahuac and dissolved its ayuntamiento or town council. A force of approximately 150 volunteers plus three coastal schooners storm the garrison at Anahuac, freeing Travis and his companions. Later Travis would become the commander of the ill-fated Alamo in San Antonio. Emboldened by their success at Anahuac over Bradburn the volunteers turned to the port of Velasco and wrested it from Mexican Lieutenant Colonel Domingo de Ugartechea and his garrison on June 25-26. The fighting at Anahuac and Velasco heralds the later Texas revolution.

December 1832. The ayuntamiento of San Antonio de Bexar meets before Christmas and publishes a list of grievances against Mexico's centralist government, then headed by President Anastasio Bustamante. These grievances, entitled *Representacion*, are additionally carried to the ayuntamientos of Goliad, Nacogdoches, Gonzales and San Felipe for their endorsement.

March 1833. Santa Anna, publicly supporting the liberal Constitution of 1824, becomes President of Mexico.

January 1834. Austin is arrested and imprisoned in Mexico City for sedition because of a letter he wrote the ayuntamiento of Bexar urging it to prepare a plan to implement separate statehood for Tejas within the Mexican federation.

May 1834. President Santa Anna announces his Plan of Cuernavaca, dissolving the Mexican Congress as well as state governments. Henceforth Santa Anna will appoint state governors. Formerly claiming to be a liberal, Santa Anna now becomes the absolute dictator of Mexico.

August 1834. Protesting Santa Anna's dictatorship and abrogation of the Constitution of 1824, Lorenzo de Zavala resigns as Mexico's minister to France. He makes his way to Tejas to join the revolutionaries.

October 1834. Juan Seguin urges Tejas ayuntamientos to send representatives to Bexar to take action against the growing powers of Santa Anna and his centralist government. The result is a document supporting the Constitution of 1824, a return to the federal system and a Tejas-wide Consultation of representatives to be held in November.

May 1835. As an example to all peoples opposing his policies Santa Anna allows his victorious troops to pillage the state of Zacatecas as well as its capital of the same name.

July 1835. Austin is released from imprisonment and returns to Texas where he is received as a hero. He and Lorenzo de Zavala head the growing Tejas insurgency.

October 1835. Townsmen and volunteers from other settlements oppose the Mexican detachment sent to Gonzales to reclaim the small cannon given the town to defend it against Indian attack. The volunteers' white flag depicts a black cannon emblazoned with the words "Come and Take It." The volunteers not only retain the cannon but fire it at the retreating Mexicans. The 100-150 Mexican dragoons led by Lieutenant Francisco Castaneda return empty-handed to San Antonio. The battle of Gonzales is often called the "Lexington of the Texas Revolution" although the volunteer victories at Anahuac and Velasco considerably preceded it.

October 1835. The battle of Concepcion between Texas revolutionaries and the Mexican army occupying San Antonio occurs at this mission just south of the town. The insurgents under Bowie, Juan Seguin and Salvador Flores are victorious.

November 1835. A quorum of representatives known as the Consultation finally convenes in San Felipe at the earlier recommendations of Lorenzo de Zavala and Juan Seguin. Purpose is to provide a provisional government, governor, general council and regular army for Tejas. The Consultation renews its support of the Mexican Constitution of 1824 and federalist government. Most delegates favor Texas' separation from the state of Coahuila but that Texas remain in the Mexican federation.

December 1835. Encouraged by his president, Santa Anna, Mexican Minister of Defense and Marine Jose Maria de Tornel issues the infamous "no quarter" decree. Promulgation of this order by Santa Anna results in the massacre of Texas prisoners at the Alamo and Goliad.

December 1835. The siege of Bexar and the occupying force of Mexican General Martin Perfecto de Cos end with a successful assault by Generals Stephen F. Austin and Edward Burleson's army. Cos surrenders, pledges never to take arms against Texas and retreats towards Mexico.

December 1835. A second Tejas/Texas declaration of independence is drafted and signed by ninety-one revolutionaries at Goliad. The signers include Tejanos Jose Miguel Aldrete and Jose Maria Jesus Carvajal. This declaration was issued without the approval, even knowledge, of the Texas provisional government.

February 1836. Mexican General Jose Urrea defeats volunteers at San Patricio, claiming twenty killed and thirty-two prisoners. Eight men escape Urrea's troops.

February 1836. Travis, Bowie, Crockett, Seguin and other volunteers occupy the Alamo as Santa Anna's 4,000-man army enters Bexar, surrounds and begins cannonading the old mission.

March 1836. General Urrea ambushes approximately fifty-two volunteers at Agua Dulce. Urrea claims forty-two killed and three captured. Five men escape the ambush, one of them is Placido Benavides. He is ordered by Doctor Grant, the volunteers' commander, to ride to Goliad to warn Fannin of Urrea's approach. As many as twenty-four of Lieutenant Benavides' men are killed at Agua Dulce making it the bloodiest Tejano battle of the war.

March 1836. The Alamo falls and all its defenders are killed in action or massacred. Among the dead are eight Tejano volunteers. Santa Anna orders all the defenders' bodies stacked and burned, except that of Tejano Gregorio Esparza who is buried elsewhere by his brother.

March 1836. Texas families are frightened by the bloody outcome at the Alamo and of Santa Anna's advance. Houston's retreat and the "runaway scrape" result. Meanwhile the Texas Convention meets at Washington-on-the-Brazos March 1, drafts a Declaration of Independence from Mexico on March 2 and delegates sign the document the following day. Among the signers are Tejanos Ruiz, Navarro and Zavala.

March 1836. General Urrea's force defeats 150 volunteers under King and Ward at Refugio.

March 1836. Almost 400 volunteers from Goliad (Presidio La Bahia) under Colonel James Fannin are caught in the open near Coleto Creek by Urrea who surrounds, defeats and takes them prisoner. On the following Palm Sunday, March 27, the prisoners are divided into three groups, each marched to a separate field and massacred in accordance with Santa Anna's express order, given in triplicate.

April 1836. After chasing Houston's army eastward to the Harrisburg vicinity, Santa Anna takes a position opposite Houston in a small field at San Jacinto. In the afternoon, the Texans launch a surprise assault and in eighteen minutes killed, wounded or routed many of Santa Anna's troops. On the left flank of Houston's assault line is Captain Juan Seguin's Tejano company which distinguishes itself. Santa Anna is later captured, forced to recognize Texas independence and orders his remaining armies out of Texas.

May 1836. Texas President David G. Burnet and Mexican President and commander of its armies, Antonio Lopez de Santa Anna, sign the two-part Treaty of Velasco, ending the war. Santa Anna's generals also sign the treaty. Once eventually returned to Mexico, Santa Anna repudiates the treaty.

1836-1845. Following the victory at San Jacinto, lawlessness and violence erupt and the livestock, homes and other properties of many Tejanos are stolen or destroyed by rampaging soldiers and civilians. To flee this undeserved, heinous treatment many flee for exile in Louisiana (as did the de Leon and Benavides families) or to Mexico (as did the Seguins). Avarice and greed reign. Many former friends and comrades ignore or forget the contributions of Tejanos to Texas independence. March 1837. Mexico announces a blockade of Texas ports. The United States recognizes the Republic of Texas.

November 1842. At Santa Anna's order, French mercenary and Mexican General Adrian Woll surprises and occupies San Antonio. This is Santa Anna's third unsuccessful foray to recover Texas. Two hundred hastily gathered volunteers defeat Woll's 1,100 regulars by luring them out of San Antonio into an ambush on the Salado Creek. The volunteers are successful and defeat Woll. However severe casualties are inflicted on fifty-two other Texans in a nearby battle called the Dawson massacre. Woll declares a victory and marches his troops back to San Antonio but starts back to Mexico the next morning. Salvador Flores organizes some 100 Tejanos participating in the battle with Woll. Antonio Menchaca, a member of Juan Seguin's company at San Jacinto, is wounded while fighting Woll in San Antonio.

December 1845. Texas is admitted to the United States to the chagrin of some Tejanos who prefer Texas become a separate state from Coahuila but remain within the Mexican federation.

LIST OF ILLUSTRATIONS

DEFINITIONS

Alcalde. The chief magistrate or mayor of a town/city.
Ajuntamiento. The town/city council.
Bexar. (also spelled Bejar). San Antonio and environs. The city of San Antonio is located in Bexar County.
Bexarenos (or Bejarenos). Citizens of San Antonio de Bexar.
Cazadore. A Mexican army rifleman.
Centralists. (or centralistas). Supporters of President/General-in-Chief Santa Anna and his policies.
Consultation. The meeting of elected representatives to discuss the future of Texas, originally suggested by Lorenzo de Zavala August 8, 1835. The Consultation eventually meets in San Felipe on October 15. One result was formation of a Permanent Council to chart an early government for Tejas.
Convention. This later group of elected representatives meets at Washington-on-the-Brazos March 1, 1836 to debate and draft the Texas Declaration of Independence from Mexico, written March 2 and signed March 3. The Convention also produces the Texas Constitution.
Deguello. Mexican martial music signalling "no quarter" for prisoners.
Execution. Putting a person to death, usually as a result of an action of a court of law.
Federalist. (or federalistas). Adherents of the Mexican Constitution of 1824 who opposed the dictatorial powers seized by President Santa Anna.
Granadero. A Mexican soldier of a grenadier unit.

Guadalupe Victoria. Center of Martin de Leon's colony on the Guadalupe River. Modern name of the town is Victoria, Texas.

Insurgents. (or revolutionaries). Tejanos, settlers, colonists, and volunteers who opposed Santa Anna.

La Bahia. The presidio or garrison at Goliad. Goliad is an anagram of the last name of Padre Hidalgo who issued the famous "Grito de Dolores" beginning the Mexican revolution against Spain.

Labor. One hundred seventy-seven acres. Many colonist heads of household were granted a league and a labor (4605 acres) of land to homestead.

League. A distance of approximately three miles or an acreage of 4,428.

Massacre. The killing of a number of usually helpless or defenseless humans under circumstances of cruelty or atrocity.

Murder. The unlawful killing of a human.

Presidio. A military post, garrison or fortress.

Pueblo. A settlement.

Ranchero. A rancher or farmer.

Regidor. A councilman of a town or city.

Slaughter. To kill large numbers of people in a violent, bloody manner.

Tejas. (or Texas) The geographical area now known as the State of Texas, formerly a part of the Mexican State of Coahuila y Tejas.

Tejanos. Spanish for Texans. A Texan of Hispanic ancestry.

Treaty. A negotiated agreement.

Victoriano. A citizen of the town of Guadalupe Victoria

Villa. A town or municipality.

Zapadore. A Mexican soldier of a sapper or pioneer unit.

CHAPTER ONE
EARLY YEARS

Call it what you like, Tejas, Texas—or as the Spanish originally did—"la tierra incognita," unknown territory. It was a wilderness comprised of vast distances of desert, mountains, llano estacado in the west, then range land separating the dry plains from forests in the east.

Spain ruled this wilderness for three hundred years. No wonder Hispanic geographical names abounded and still do. These great expanses were not accurately mapped until 1519.

Originally there were few settlements in Tejas, each with its own protecting military garrison or presidio against Indian attack. The largest settlements were San Antonio de Bexar, La Bahia or Goliad, and the easternmost town on the fringes of the United States, Nacogdoches. There were estimated to be only 7,000 inhabitants or Tejanos.[1]

Who were the Tejanos? Originally they were the old Mexican families granted lands north of the Rio Grande River by the Spanish royal government. Others drifted north from "New Spain" or Mexico to stake their claims for land. Early families worked hard, establishing homes, farms and ranches, prospering, as did their descendents, native-born Tejanos.

Revolution and reprisal have been an integral part of Tejano legacy. First there were hardships meted out by the Spanish royalist army from 1813-1823, then by Antonio Lopez de Santa Anna's Mexican army in 1835-1836, finally by soldiers of fortune and unscrupulous businessmen lured from the United States by the promise of cheap

1

lands during the period following Texas independence. Through it all, Tejanos endured.

Tejas land was the most viable currency since there was little else of known value in la tierra incognita. The first permanent settlement was established in 1681 after the Pueblo Indians drove the Spanish south toward present day El Paso, Texas (originally known as El Paso del Norte). Nearby, two small missions, Ysleta del Sur and Socorro del Sur were established. Ysleta is considered the oldest European settlement in Texas.

In 1690 the mission San Francisco de las Tejas was founded much farther to the east in what is now Houston County, Texas. And in 1700 another mission, San Juan Bautista, was moved near the Rio Grande River, close to present day Eagle Pass, Texas. San Juan Bautista became a major gateway to Tejas from Mexico.

Jose de Escandon was authorized by the Spanish king in 1746 to improve and organize the previously haphazard colonization by planning settlements throughout the area. Tomas Sanchez received a land grant along the Rio Grande River in 1751 from which Laredo, Texas developed.

Many other small Tejas communities sprang up beside the Rio Grande in the lower valley as a result of Escandon's prodigious efforts. Familiar names today include Laredo, Mier, Camargo, Reynosa and Revilla. Many old families in modern-day Texas hold titles to their lands based on original grants from this early period.

Escandon also encouraged settlers to begin livestock ranching. In 1753 he granted Captain Jose Vasquiz Borrego 433,800 acres in which to develop his ranch in present day Zapata County, Texas.

In 1765 Jose de Galvez was dispatched to New Spain—an area encompassing all of modern Mexico plus much of the American west—and instructed to improve both the economy and the defenses of that vast area. Known as Spain's greatest colonial administrator, he reorganized the tax system, formed a government tobacco monopoly and expanded commerce.[2]

To the east, Edward Murphy was granted a land grant by the Spanish government in 1791 and he encouraged several families from the United States to become squatters near Nacogdoches.[3]

A 1795 census gauged the success of Spain's efforts to develop its tierra incognita holdings. There were reported to be sixty-nine families living on forty-five ranches in the San Antonio area alone. An 1803 census estimated there were 100,000 head of cattle in Tejas.

The first Tejano to formally declare Tejas independence from Spain was republican Bernardo Gutierrez de Lara in April 1813. Long an opponent of the Spaniards, de Lara successively fought the royalists at Nacogoches, La Bahia (Goliad) and Bexar (San Antonio). At the latter he issued the first declaration of independence of Tejas. He wrote "We are free and independent and have the right to the establishment of our own government." De Lara's short-lived title was "President Protector of the Provisional Government of the State of Texas."[4]

In August 1813, the first Tejas revolution ended with a Spanish royalist victory over the republicans at the battle of the Medina. Some 1,000 republican troops were slain. To further terrorize any liberal-leaning Tejanos, the Spanish publicly executed every tenth prisoner in the military plaza of San Antonio.

Commended for his part in the battle and the bloody execution, without trial, of republican prisoners was a young royalist army lieutenant named Antonio Lopez de Santa Anna who would become the Mexican president and general-in-chief known for his cruelty to prisoners at the Alamo and Goliad.

Tejano Jose Antonio Navarro, a republican, escaped to Louisiana after the battle of Medina with the Spanish. Like de Lara, he would become a signer of a declaration of independence, this one the Texas Declaration of Independence from Mexico drafted March 2, 1865. Yet another Tejano escaping from the royalists was Navarro's uncle, Jose Francisco Ruiz, also a future signer of the Texas Declaration.[5]

Indians were the first immigrant group from the United States coming to Tejas. As early as 1818, Cherokees from the southeastern United States settled north of Nacogdoches on lands between the Trinity and Sabine rivers. The Cherokees were quickly followed by a second and much larger wave of diverse, mostly Anglo settlers attracted by Tejas lands.

Acting for the Spanish government, Governor Antonio M. Martinez of San Antonio approved the colonization request of Moses Austin, the father of Stephen F. Austin, in January 1821. The elder Austin's plan was to bring three hundred families to a colony located between the Brazos and Colorado Rivers. The death of Moses Austin and the defeat and expulsion of the Spanish by the new and independent Mexico in 1821 delayed the fulfillment of Moses' plan by his son.

Stephen F. Austin arrived in Tejas in July 1821 to fulfill his father's deathbed request to complete the colonization contract. Two Tejanos, Erasmo Seguin and J.M.J. Veramendi, friends of his father, provided young Stephen with advice and assistance upon his arrival in San Antonio de Bexar. Thanks to their mentoring, Stephen's early efforts to get his colony started—and his acceptance by Bejarenos—were successful.

Erasmo (sometimes spelled Erasmus) Seguin was elected alcalde or mayor of San Antonio in 1820. Such was his popularity and ability that he was made postmaster in 1822, then the quartermaster of Bexar in 1825. Erasmo, father of Juan Nepomuceno Seguin, established a large ranch called La Mora and fortified it against Indian attacks. In 1821 he was selected by the governor of Coahuila to inform Moses Austin that his land grant had been approved. The friendship between the elder Seguin and young Stephen F. Austin lasted for fifteen years, encompassing the political and financial as well as personal aspects of both.[6]

In January, 1823 the Spanish grant originally given Moses Austin was approved by the Mexican government, allowing Stephen F. Austin to bring in the designated families known as the "Old Three Hundred." More grants were given and more settlers from the Unites States came to Tejas.

Martin de Leon y Galvan was another empresario who, like Austin, founded a colony in Tejas. His earlier petitions to the Spanish government were rebuffed several times because he was rumored to be disloyal to Spain. Mexican independence from Spain in 1821 began an era of more tolerant colonization policies. In April 1824, de Leon petitioned for permission to settle forty-one families from the Mexican State of Tamaulipas at a place he named Nuestra Senora de Guadalupe de Jesus. His charter was approved the same month and he moved settlers into the designated area between the Guadalupe and Lavaca rivers.[7]

Present-day Victoria, Texas, the center of the de Leon colony, was named for the first president of Mexico, Jesus Guadalupe de Victoria, a personal friend of Martin de Leon.

Martin became an immensely successful rancher and businessman and was the first to use a cattle brand in Tejas. The brand was a connected E and J, representing "Espiritu de Jesus." His innovations and industry provided the foundations of Tejas' highly successful cattle industry. He died following the cholera epidemic of 1833 but his family continued his legacy. Several de Leon family members served on Goliad's ayuntamiento or town council. Two served as alcaldes of Goliad and another was commandant of the nearby La Bahia presidio.[8]

The son of Erasmo Seguin, Juan, followed in his father's public service footsteps at the early age of 22. Juan was elected one of San Antonio's two regidores or aldermen in 1829. He also filled in for Gaspar Flores, the Bexar alcalde, during the latter's absence.

Empresario Stephen Austin was busily settling immigrants into his colony, centered at San Felipe de Austin on the Brazos River. By 1824, he had issued 222 land titles.

But 1824 is more important as the date of the Mexican Constitution establishing the liberal pattern of government for Mexico until Antonio Lopez de Santa Anna usurped it. This important document, the first of the new and independent Mexico, is the divining rod between liberals who supported the Constitution and centralists, its opponents.

Between resolving disputes among his "family" of settlers and mollifying tempers between settlers and Mexican officials, Austin found time to draft a constitution for Mexico along with a "plan of federal government." He submitted them to Jose Miguel Ramos Arispe (also spelled Arizpe) often called the father of Mexican federalism.

Arispe represented Coahuila in the Spanish Cortes or parliament, then returned to Mexico in 1822. He also studied the Spanish Constitution as well as Austin's plan. Six months later statesman Arispe had completed his "acta constitutiva" which provided the framework for the Constitution of 1824.[9]

Due to the Constitution of 1824's impact on all subsequent events in Tejas, it is repeated in its original, translated wording at Appendix A.

Another Mexican liberal statesman whose name would later resound throughout Tejas was the President of the Mexican Congress that approved the Constitution of 1824. His name, Lorenzo de Zavala, was the first to appear on that document. He would later emerge in Tejas as a respected voice of liberals defending the Constitution against the wiles of President and General-in-Chief Antonio Lopez de Santa Anna.

The Constitution of 1824 was similar to portions of that of the United States. But historian Alesso Vito Robles differs and wrote "the conception of the one and the other differ absolutely."[10]

One difference is Title 1-3. "The Religion of the Mexican Nation is, and will be perpetually, the Roman Catholic Apostolic. The Nation will protect it by wise and just laws, and prohibit the exercise of any other whatever."

There were several common aspects. Title 2-4 reads "The Mexican Nation adopts for its Government, the form of Republican representative, popular Federal." Title 2-6Y indicates "The supreme power of the Federation will be divided for its exercise, in Legislative, Executive, and Judicial."

Title 3-7 provides for a General Congress of two parts, "one of Deputies (Representatives) and the other of Senators."

On March 12, 1825 Austin assembled his colonists at San Felipe de Austin and read them Mexico's new constitution. The militia then fired a twenty-three gun salute to the states and provinces of Mexico, the state of Coahuila y Tejas being one. Afterwards Austin led the assemblage in an oath of allegiance to Mexico.[11]

One of Austin's constant reminders to his settlers was that they owed "fidelity and gratitude to Mexico." At the time, Austin preferred Tejas become a separate state within the Mexican federation, a preference shared by many Tejanos. Austin wrote "You may say that Texas needs a government, and that the best she can have, is to be created a State in the Mexican federation."[12]

Tejanos fought for the independence of Tejas long before Stephen F. Austin and his host of settlers arrived. An example is Bernardo Gutierrez de Lara who defeated the Spanish royalists at the three largest Tejas settlements, Nacogdoches, Goliad and San Antonio. De Lara was the first to declare the independence of Tejas.

Also fighting the royalists were Navarro and Ruiz, later both would sign the 1836 Texas Declaration of Independence from Mexico. Erasmo Seguin exemplified political leadership in San Antonio. Martin de Leon was among the first empresarios developing Tejas economically. Lorenzo de Zavala resigned as Mexican minister to France, protesting

Santa Anna's dictatorship, then moved to Tejas to lead liberals there. "I am now a colonist in the province of Texas," he announced proudly.

In the absence of the imprisoned Austin, Zavala began meeting Tejanos, colonists and settlers concerned about their diminishing liberties under Santa Anna's new centralist system. Zavala became an interim Stephen F. Austin, providing leadership to Texans concerned about liberty.

TEXAS VICE PRESIDENT LORENZO de ZAVALA
An author of the Mexican Constitution of 1824, he advocated
its application to Tejas, along with Stephen F. Austin. A
signer of the Texas Declaration of Independence, Zavala
also helped write the Texas Constitution.
(courtesy of Texas State Library & Archives Commission)

CHAPTER TWO
DISCONTENT INCREASES

Most Tejanos approved of the influx of settlers from the United States since new immigrants improved the local economy and defenses against persistent Indian attacks. Generally, the two groups—Tejanos and the newly arrived settlers—got along well despite cultural, religious and language differences.

"The only significant area of disagreement concerned the proper way to present grievances to the Mexican government."[1]

The newcomers called conventions to discuss problems and draft petitions to Mexico City requesting changes. The Tejanos preferred that grievances emanate from civil authorities.

Relations were more tenuous in the Nacogdoches area where Hayden Edwards was empresario. In December 1826 thirty dissatisfied settlers under the leadership of Hayden's brother, Benjamin, revolted against the Mexican authorities' rules and regulations. The rebels declared themselves the independent "Fredonian Republic." Empresario Stephen Austin feared the Fredonians would cause Mexican authorities to harshly react against his own fragile colony. Extolling fidelity to Mexico, Austin led a militia company north against the Fredonians. Their revolt lasted only six weeks and peace was restored.

By 1830 more than 25 empresarios had been commissioned by the Mexican government to settle colonists. That same year Tejas attained an estimated population of 15,000. The United States arrivals were four times as numerous as the Tejanos.[2]

That same year Austin's colony numbered 4,000. The increasing number of settlers coming from the United States "bewildered" some Tejanos who began to lose interest in Mexican affairs. One observer lamented that his fellow Tejanos knew little about the revolution in Mexico and were adopting the habits and customs of the newcomers. He continued that many Tejanos were only "Mexicans by birth" and even spoke Spanish with "noticeable error."[3]

Like 1824, the year 1830 was doubly significant because of new legislation from the Mexican Congress. Its law of April 6, 1830 halted further immigration from the Unites States, including slaves, and began the collection of customs fees from all non-Mexican commercial ships. More control was needed Mexico City reasoned, as proven by the unsettling Fredonian uprising in Nacogdoches. Customs houses supported by Mexican army detachments were established at several Texas ports.

Two Mexican officials were ordered to establish themselves and the new government controls preventing further immigration and begin the collection of customs fees. An important seven-year customs exemption on goods arriving at Texas ports expired in 1830.

George Fisher, originally from Serbia, arrived in Brazoria in May 1830 to open a customs house at that port on the Gulf coast. Fisher began collecting fees of $2.125 per ton from non-Mexican vessels. Alarmed by the trade damage the fees were causing, Austin and others decried Fisher to General Mier y Teran, Fisher's superior in Matamoros, Mexico. The clamor convinced the general to withdraw Fisher, at least temporarily.

Later in the year an army garrison was established at Anahuac at the far end of the bay opposite the island of Galveston. Commander of that garrison was Lieutenant Colonel John or Juan Davis Bradburn, born in Virginia but raised in Kentucky, now a Mexican army officer. Bradburn closed the Brazoria port and began collecting fees at Anahuac. Texans complained loudly enough for Bradburn to reopen the Brazoria port.

Unpopular George Fisher returned to the Texas coast, this time to take Bradburn's position at Anahuac. Fisher began requiring ship captains arriving at Texas ports to present papers to him at Anahuac before sailing. For example, if a non-Mexican ship landed at Brazoria, its skipper had to make the one hundred mile overland trip to Anahuac for Fisher's permission to legally set sail from Brazoria.

In February 1832 Austin's colony petitioned the Mexican government to repeal the April 6, 1830 immigration ban, renewal of the former customs exemption and, of course, dismissal of George Fisher.

Not to be outdone by Fisher, Bradburn arrested several old settlers, among them Francisco Madero, the land commissioner, as well as some new arrivals including William B. Travis, the future commander of the Alamo, for violations of the Law of April 1830. Locals were inflamed by several other Bradburn actions and stormed the garrison at Anahuac, supported by three coastal schooners. At least one Tejano, Damacio Ximenes (also spelled Jimenez), fought at the battle of Anahuac. "After some fighting, the enemy surrendered, the redoubtable Bradburn making his escape by night and fleeing into Louisiana."[4]

Encouraged by the easy success against the Mexican garrison at Anahuac, some 112 settlers attacked another—this one at Velasco—on the night of June 25, 1832. Their land attack was supported by another schooner whose deck was lined with riflemen. The garrison of 150 soldiers under Mexican Lieutenant Colonel Domingo de Ugartechea raised the white flag of surrender the next morning. Ugartechea convinced his captors that he was an ardent liberal supporting the Constitution of 1824 so was allowed to march his troops south to Matamoros. Casualty reports from this bloody encounter between the Mexican army and the settlers differ. One claims Mexican casualties as thirty-five killed and fifteen wounded. It also reported Texas losses were seven killed and twenty-seven wounded.[5]

Among the insurgents killed was one Tejano whose name was not recorded.

The struggles at Anahuac and Velasco were the opening rounds of hostilities between the Mexican government and Tejas colonists and settlers. The more famous, later battle over the Gonzales cannon is sometimes called the "Lexington" of the Texas revolutionary struggle. But the battle at Gonzales was still several years away. The first armed struggles of the Texas revolution were at Anahuac and Velasco.

Shortly before Christmas 1832, the ayuntamiento or city council of San Antonio de Bexar published *Representacion*, a list of grievances against the Mexican government. It shared this important document with ayuntamientos in Goliad, Gonzales, Nacodoches and San Felipe, requesting their endorsements.

A local committee in Nacogoches met January 26, 1833 and endorsed *Representacion* with two additions. One was that the ten year customs exemption on landed goods be extended to goods brought overland through Nacogoches. The other was that foreigners of good repute settled in the Nacogoches area receive clear title to their lands.

"Dated December 19, 1832, *Representacion* was the only published statement of major issues affecting Texas and of Tejanos' misgivings about their centralist government."[6]

More specifically *Representacion* detailed Bexareno grievances against an increasing authoritarian Mexican government that had abrogated the federal principles of the Constitution of 1824. Among other complaints were the government's failure to protect Tejas against a new Comanche uprising and to pay its troops and militia. The Law of April 6, 1830 banning further immigration from the Unites States was itself in violation of the Constitution of 1824, it claimed. Also cited was the government's manipulation of land prices discouraging immigration from Mexico. Texas land was available for 300 pesos per acre while in neighboring Coahuila, the price was only 15 pesos.

Although Austin and other empresarios supported the ideals of the *Representacion*, it began as an initiative of Tejanos not the newcomers.

In March 1833, Antonio Lopez de Santa Anna seized power from President Anastasio Bustamante and reversed his political compass. Earlier Santa Anna had claimed to be a liberal fully supportive of the Constitution of 1824. Suddenly he became the absolute dictator of Mexico and usurper of that constitution. His actions caused rising concern in Texas as well as several Mexican states, especially Zacatecas and Yucatan.

In April alarmed Texans called a meeting in San Felipe to draft a constitution for an independent state of Tejas within the Mexican federation. Austin was chosen by the convention to journey to Mexico City to present this proposal and others to the Mexican government. He arrived in Mexico City in July and spent several months unsuccessfully arguing for separate Mexican statehood for Texas, repeal of the Law of April 1830 and free trade.

Discouraged by his lack of progress, Austin wrote an October letter to the San Antonio ayuntamiento urging it and all Tejas ayuntamientos to prepare a plan for independent statehood "even though the general government withholds its consent."[7]

He succeeded in convincing the Mexican government to repeal that portion of the Law of April 1830 eliminating immigration from the Unites States. The proposal to recognize Tejas as an independent state within the Mexican federation was rejected. In December a discouraged Austin left Mexico City on his way back to Tejas. Enroute he was arrested and returned to Mexico City where he was imprisoned for sedition. His letter to the Bexar ayuntamiento had reached the desk of Mexican Vice President (acting President) Gomez Farias, who enraged, ordered Austin's arrest.

Meanwhile, President Santa Anna promulgated his May 1834 Plan of Cuernavaca, codifying his changes in the Mexican government. He dissolved the liberal Congress, installed his own centralists, abolished state governments, making them departments and reserving for himself the appointment of their heads.

Santa Anna's minister to France was Lorenzo de Zavala who had presided over the Mexican Congress that drafted the Constitution of 1824. Zavala had been the first to sign that document, preemptively set aside by Santa Anna. In protest Zavala resigned his position and headed toward Texas, despite orders for his arrest and return to Mexico City.

Another Mexican republican leader, Senator Jose Antonio Mexia, vigorously opposed Santa Anna's actions and organized a resistance. Eventually Mexia was captured and executed by the centralists.

Juan Seguin, son of Erasmo, urged municipal leaders to send representatives to San Antonio in October 1834 to confer about Santa Anna's moves and develop possible courses of action. This was the first attempt to organize liberal, federalist opponents of Santa Anna in Texas. The initiator was a Tejano. One result was a declaration by forty-nine citizens supporting the Constitution of 1824 and a system of federal—instead of centralist—government.

In the capital and state of Zacatecas, a revolt against Santa Anna's policies was fermenting. A new law passed by Santa Anna's congress limited the size of state militias. The liberal governor of Zacatecas refused to decrease his militia strength estimated at 4000 men but probably considerably less in reality. The Zacatecans dug defensive trenches east of the neighboring town of Guadalupe and prepared for onslaught by Santa Anna's force of 2500 regulars.

Masking his attack plan by burning many campfires opposite the Zacatecan militia trenches, Santa Anna flanked those positions and attacked from the south. The silver-rich capital city of Zacatecas fell May 11,1835. Santa Anna permitted his victorious troops to pillage and rob throughout the state and its capital. Several foreigners in the capital were killed and the Mexican government eventually paid indemnity to the British.

The frightening news of Santa Anna's rewarding his troops with two days of rape and looting of foreigners as well as citizens of Zacatecas for their resistance echoed throughout Tejas. The sack of Zacatecas was a poignant warning to others of the severity and cruelty to be meted out to opponents of their centralist government.

Yet another enemy of Santa Anna's repressive policies was the governor of the state of Coahuila y Tejas, Augustin Viesca. He published a June 1835 handbill warning Texans of the dangers of centralism. It began "Citizens of Texas, arise in arms or sleep forever! Thy dearest interests, thy liberty, thy properties, what is more, thy very existence depends upon the deceitful capriciousness of the most malevolent enemies. Thy destruction is already resolved, and only thy firmness and thy special energy can save thee!"[8]

Viesca's handbill excited little reaction in Tejas where his government had lost credibility, particularly among the new arrivals. Among Viesca's problems was the controversy over whether the capital of Coahuila y Tejas should be Saltillo or Monclova. Viesca later escaped from Santa Anna's imprisonment and joined the resistance at Goliad.

Following Governor Viesca's proclamation, Lorenzo de Zavala, once Santa Anna's minister to France and an advocate of federalism and the Constitution of 1824, toured settlements in Texas voicing his concerns about the fate of Texas under Santa Anna. At Harrisburg, he spoke against the centralist program of the Mexican government. By July 15 he was in Brazoria meeting with William H. Wharton and others espousing independence. Wharton later became the Republic of Texas' minister to the United States.

In August Zavala was to attend a Lynch's Ferry meeting at which he was invited to speak. Illness prevented him from going to Lynch's Ferry but he provided a message to be read there which contained his summation of the rights and duties of Texas citizens. His letter also contained a recommendation that an October 15 "Consultation" be assembled for Texas representatives to discuss their future.

The same day Zavala's message was read at Lynch's Ferry an order was issued by Mexican General Perfecto de Cos for Zavala's arrest and return to Matamoros. News of Cos' action spread throughout Texas, strengthening settlers' opinion of the outspoken Mexican liberal, now a Texan. The populace of Columbia met August 15 and adopted a fiery resolution that "We will not give up any individual to the military authorities."[9]

The actions of the citizens of Columbia, refusing to give up an individual to Mexican authorities, followed a similar refusal by the citizens of Guadalupe Victoria. In June 1835 under the leadership of alcalde Placido Benavides, they refused to allow the arrest of Jose Maria Jesus Carbajal, a staunch proponent of the Constitution of 1824, by Santa Anna's cavalry.

On August 15 a "Committee of Safety and Correspondence" formed in Columbia called for a Consultation of delegates representing all Texas to meet on October 15 per Zavala's suggestion.

Santa Anna became an ardent critic of Zavala once the latter chose to be a Tejas colonist rather than Santa Anna's minister to France. "Some Mexicans," he wrote, "partisans of a former system of government, thought, perhaps in good faith, that the only effect of fanning the fire of war in Texas would be a political change in accord with their opinion. Their shortsighted ambition must be a terrible lesson to them as well as a source of eternal remorse."[10]

Austin, the generally recognized leader of Texas, was still imprisoned in Mexico City. In his place, newly arrived Lorenzo de Zavala stoked Texans' enthusiasm for concerted action to preserve their rights against the tyrant, President Antonio Lopez de Santa Anna.

REVOLUTIONARY TEJAS

N

(1 inch = approx. 100 miles)

GULF OF MEXICO

MEXICO

USA

RIVERS
1 - Sabine
2 - Brazos
3 - Colorado
4 - Guadalupe
5 - San Antonio
6 - Nueces
7 - Rio Grande

BATTLE SITES, OTHER LOCATIONS
A - Nacogdoches
B - Anahuac
C - Lynch's Ferry
D - San Jacinto
E - Galveston
F - Washington-on-the-Brazos
G - San Felipe
H - Harrisburg
I - Velasco
J - Gonzales
K - Victoria
L - San Antonio
M - The Alamo
N - Mission Concepcion
P - Goliad
O - Refugio
Q - Copano
R - San Patricio
S - Agua Dulce
T - Matamoros

CHAPTER THREE
COME AND TAKE IT

Austin was released from his Mexico City imprisonment in July and boarded a ship bound for New Orleans, then another for Texas. Due to his long imprisonment and disillusionment with Santa Anna, he abandoned his previous dictum to his settlers, "Fidelity and Gratitude to Mexico," on the pier at Vera Cruz.

By September 12 Austin was back in Texas and had accepted the leadership of the Consultation initiated by Zavala's earlier recommendation. The two shared identical misgivings about Santa Anna and the future of Texas under his centralist system. By the end of September, Zavala and Austin were working and living together in San Felipe, the center of Austin's colony.

From Austin's role as the chairman of the Committee of Safety and Correspondence to the command of Texas' ragtag army was a short step. In October the Gonzales community in the DeWitt colony called upon Austin for military assistance. In Austin's absence Zavala became the chairman of the San Felipe central committee.[1]

In October 2, 1835 a battle between the Mexican army and rebellious Texans took place near Gonzales. Some historians describe this event as the first shot of the revolution or as the "Lexington of Texas." However, battles at Anahuac and Velasco preceded that at Gonzales by several years.

Colonel Domingo de Ugartechea—who earlier fought, surrendered and been paroled at Velasco by the insurgents—had been promoted, returned to Texas and posted to San Antonio as its garrison commander.

He sent Corporal DeLeon and five soldados to recover a small cannon loaned to the citizens of Gonzales for protection against Indian attack. DeLeon's request for the cannon was quickly refused, several of his men disarmed and the disorganized group began trudging back to Bexar.

Eighteen citizens of Gonzales, now memorialized as the "Original Old Gonzales 18" stood at the riverbank and refused to surrender the small cannon. Among those eighteen was Tejano Benjamin Fuqua, whose nephew, Galba, would become at least equally famous at the Alamo.

When Corporal DeLeon's unsuccessful excursion became known, Ugarechea dispatched Lieutenant Francisco Castaneda with over a hundred dragoons to recover the Gonzales cannon from the insurgents. The cannon was described as a small bronze six-pound cannon. The cannon had been requested by empresario Green DeWitt who, like Stephen F. Austin, had brought a colony of settlers to Tejas. The 1831 receipt for the cannon described it as a "reinforced bronze cannon." It was in need of repair as a result of a spike being driven into the touchhole of the cannon to disable it.

The lieutenant's difficult mission was to avoid a confrontation yet recover the cannon, arrest the Gonzales alcalde and any other resistors, returning them to San Antonio as prisoners.[2]

Lieutenant Castaneda arrived on the western bank of the Guadalupe River opposite Gonzales. His scouts discovered all rafts, boats and barges for crossing the river had been removed by the settlers who refused to surrender their cannon. Hearing of the confrontation and impending battle, volunteers from all over Tejas began gathering at Gonzales. Above them flew a white flag sewed the night before by Sarah DeWitt, wife of empresario Green DeWitt, and other ladies. It depicted the outline of a small cannon with the challenge "Come and Take It" surmounted by the outline of a single star

A message sent from Gonzales' citizens to San Felipe and other towns read "A detachment of Mexican forces from Bexar (San Antonio) amounting to about one hundred and fifty men, are encamped opposite us; we expect an attack momentarily. Yesterday we were but 18 strong, to day 150 & forces constantly arriving. We wish all the aid and despatch that is possible to give us that we may take up soon our line of march for Bexar and drive from our country all the Mexican forces."[3]

One responder to Gonzales' request for assistance was Placido Benavides, the alcalde of Guadalupe Victoria who organized a company of some twenty-eight ranchers from the Victoria area, but arrived too late. Initially Benavides wanted to capture Mexican General Cos, newly landed at Copano Bay. He changed his plans and joined other volunteers marching to liberate Goliad/La Bahia on October 10.

Juan Sequin was commissioned a captain in the "Federal Army of Texas" on October 23, 1835 and recruited a company to be provided weapons and ammunition by the provisional government. Salvador Flores became Seguin's first lieutenant. Flores and Manuel Leal (also called Manuel Tarin) organized forty-one Tejano volunteers into a company from ranches southwest of San Antonio and deployed it against the Mexicans at Salado Creek. Later, Lieutenant Flores was commended by General Austin for his bravery and actions on the Salado.

By then Juan Seguin and Placido Benavides were organizing another unit of some seventy men to support Austin. Salvador Flores became first lieutenant of the Bexar contingent and Placido Benavides the first lieutenant of the Goliad volunteers.[4]

Andrew Ponton, the alcalde of Gonzales, had polled its citizens and all but three voted to keep the their cannon which Urgartechea claimed was needed for the defense of San Antonio. Ponton wisely began preparing his people for trouble, moving some families to safer areas, gathering weapons and provisions and sending messengers to surrounding settlements for assistance. They also buried the small cannon in a peach orchard in case their defenses failed.

Castaneda requested a meeting with the alcalde but was told across the river by regidor or councilman Joseph Clements that the alcalde was not available. Clements added that he would be available at 4:00 p.m. that afternoon to represent the alcalde, if the latter was still unavailable.

During the night of September 29, Lieutenant Castaneda moved his position to higher ground some 300 yards from the river. Aware of the growing strength of the DeWitt settlers and volunteers, Castaneda again moved his detachment to a more defensible position seven miles from Gonzales on the morning of October 1.

Three citizens dug up the cannon on October 1, hastily repaired it, mounted it on wooden wagon wheels and gathered small pieces of scrap metal that would fit into the cannon's muzzle. They loaded the cannon with 16 inches of black powder, then the scrap metal pieces.

That night, October 1, the settlers and volunteers went on the offensive and crossed the Guadalupe at the Gonzales ferry with about fifty cavalrymen, the cannon and a number of foot soldiers to service the cannon and provide a rear guard.

The Gonzales volunteers cautiously searched for the Mexican positions in a dense fog early on the morning of October 2. A barking dog alerted the Mexican pickets who fired into the fog, wounding one Texan.

When the fog lifted about 9:00 a.m. the Texans began firing on the Mexicans now visible some 350 yards away. Firing stopped and a parley between the two commanders was agreed upon. After an inconclusive meeting of the Mexican and Texan commanders in an open field, each returned to their positions. Cannoneer J.C. Neill was ordered to fire the now famous Gonzales cannon, which was followed by a rifle volley and charge by the settlers and volunteers. Lieutenant Castaneda began withdrawing back toward San Antonio with one or two casualties and without the little cannon.

After the successful siege and assault of Bexar in December 1835 the Gonzales six-pounder may have been taken to the Alamo to add to its defenses. Reportedly it was one of the twenty-one cannon deployed against Santa Anna's army. After the fall of the Alamo the Gonzales cannon, along with many others, may have been melted down by the Mexican army. For a different version concerning the cannon's history, see Appendix G.

Nearby on the ranch of Salvador Flores, a volunteer group of Tejano ranchers met with Juan Seguin and Flores to declare their support of the revolution. Flores would serve in the Texas army from 1835 to 1836, attaining the rank of captain.[5]

Juan Seguin would become one of the most famous leaders of the revolution, eventually becoming a colonel in the Texas army.

Meanwhile Zavala was elected Harrisburg's representative to the Texas-wide Consultation that initially met on October 17. Lacking a quorum, the Consultation was postponed until November 1. Pending that date, Zavala became a member of the Permanent Council, the interim government of Texas.

Prominent Tejano families provided generous aid to Austin's Texas "army." Martin de Leon's family, now headed by Fernando, donated $35,000 worth of horses, mules, cattle, equipment and provisions for the army. The de Leon family contributed its men as well as its money and materiel. Jose Maria Jesus Carbajal, who later became a Mexican general, and Placido Benavides, a Texas captain, were de Leon sons-in-law.[6]

Dona Patricia de la Garza de Leon, wife of Martin de Leon, attempted to smuggle arms and ammunition from New Orleans for the Texas army. Maria Antonio de la Garza of Victoria offered sixty beeves to feed the revolutionaries now headed by General Stephen F. Austin.[7]

Gonzales provided the catalyst for the growth of the Texas army, described as untrained, undisciplined and meagerly supplied. "Come and Take It" evoked a spirit uniting Tejanos, settlers and volunteers in a common cause: march on San Antonio de Bexar and Goliad to expel Santa Anna's Mexican army from Texas.

THE GONZALES "COME AND TAKE IT" CANNON
The cannon which Gonzales settlers and volunteers refused
to surrender to Mexican forces September-October 1835.
(photo courtesy of N.K. Rogers)

SEGUIN'S STATUE IN SEGUIN, TEXAS

A portion of the inscriptions reads "Juan Nepomuceno Seguin, October 27, 1806-August 27, 1889. I embraced the cause of Texas at the report of the first cannon which foretold her liberty, filled an honorable situation in the ranks of the conquerors of San Jacinto, and was a member of the Legislative body of the Republic." (photo courtesy of N.K. Rogers)

CHAPTER FOUR
RETAKING GOLIAD AND SAN ANTONIO DE BEXAR

In late September, General Perfecto de Cos, brother-in-law of Santa Anna, landed five hundred troops at Copano Bay on the Texas coast. He had been ordered by Santa Anna to bring order to insurgent, unruly Texas. Cos and his centralista troops quickly offended Texans by their attitude and activities. An example was the public whipping of the Goliad alcalde by a Mexican officer. The alcalde was punished because he did not act quickly enough to procure carts to transport General Cos' extensive personal baggage.[1]

Reacting to the insurgents' victory at Gonzales, Cos marched out of Goliad on October 5, leaving only a detachment for security. The customs collector at Goliad was Tejano Juan Zentano who sent a message to Philip Dimitt's (also spelled Dimmitt) group along the Lavaca River that Cos had departed Goliad with his main force, leaving stay-behinds to secure the presidio. A Texas attack there might be successful, Zentano opined.[2]

Arriving back in Guadalupe Victoria, Benavides and his thirty riders joined George M. Collingsworth's Matagorda volunteers intent on liberating Goliad/La Bahia. The Collingsworth force stopped in Victoria to rest. There forty-nine of the volunteers, including Juan Antonio Padilla, Jose Maria Jesus Carbajal and A. Constanza, promised area locals they would be protected from the Mexican military if the locals would remain loyal to the Constitution of 1824.

The Collingsworth force moved out and arrived in Goliad on the night of October 9. The town sponsored a dance that night in an attempt to lure the Mexican commander and his officers out of the garrison before Collingsworth's planned attack. The wary Mexican commander, Lieutenant Colonel Francisco Sandoval, became suspicious and left the dance early with his officers. Collingsworth then sent Juan Antonio Padilla and three others to demand the surrender of the presidio. Sandoval refused. The insurgents attacked and captured La Bahia the next day.[3]

Although unpopular among many Tejanos, Dimitt was elected captain by the Goliad insurgents and left in charge of the captured presidio. Prominent Tejanos in Dimitt's force were Jose Miguel Aldrete (sometimes spelled Alderete), Jose Maria Jesus Carbajal, Placido Benavides and Juan Antonio Padilla. Dimitt also relied on the scouting ability of three members of the same family—the Escaleros—Juan, Jose Maria and Manuel. The Tejanos also were of inestimable value to Dimitt by helping safely evacuate families, Tejano and otherwise, from the Goliad-Refugio war zone.

Captain Seguin wrote "On the 13th of October I met Austin on the Salado (Creek) and joined my forces with his small army. Upon this occasion, I had the honor of being acquainted with General Sam Houston, who accompanied Austin. On the same day, we had a slight engagement with the forces under Cos, who retired into San Antonio. Austin, as the commander-in-chief of the army, gave me the appointment of captain."[4]

On October 14 Benavides and his approximately thirty men complied with General Austin's order to join his army near San Antonio to scout the town occupied by Mexican General Perfecto de Cos and approximately 1200 troops.

Meanwhile Seguin and Placido Benavides were organizing another seventy men to support Austin's siege and attack on San Antonio de Bexar. Salvador Flores was elected first lieutenant of the Bexar men; Placido Benavides as the first lieutenant of the Goliad contingent.

Flores' assignment was to reconnoiter the four old Cathoic missions on the southern outskirts of San Antonio in the company of Bowie, Fannin and Seguin. The names of these missions (and the years of their establishment) are San Jose y San Miguel de Aguayo (1720), San Juan Capistrano (1731), Nuestra Senora de la Purisima Concepcion de Acuna (1755), and San Francisco de la Espada (1756).[5]

Captain Seguin was charged with foraging food and provisions for Austin's hungry, poorly equipped army. Without the support of ranchers like his father, Erasmo, Jose Antonio Navarro and Jose Maria Solmos, Seguin's mission might have failed. The ability of the army to maintain its siege of San Antonio would have been jeopardized without the corn, beans, beef, salt and forage Seguin scrounged.

Seguin, after meeting Austin on Salado Creek, was ordered to accompany his friend, Jim Bowie, on an October 27 patrol. With ninety-two men they examined Mission San Francisco de la Espada, then Mission San Juan, then Mission San Jose y San Miguel de Aguayo. All were deemed indefensible. The group, joined by Captain William Travis, who would become the final commander at the Alamo, and Lieutenant Salvador Flores eventually arrived at Mission Nuestra Senora de la Purisima Concepcion de Acuna which was selected as General Austin's base of operations against San Antonio/Bexar. Mission Concepcion is about two miles south of the town.

General Cos was swift to act on his scouts' reports concerning the insurgents' movements and dispatched four hundred soldiers of the Morales Division to attack them at Mission Concepcion. The Morales Division, also known as the "Invincibles," contained infantry, cavalry and a six-pound cannon.

Despite an early morning dense fog on October 28, Cos ordered the attack against the Bowie/Fannin force positioned on an east bank curve of the San Antonio River. The insurgents' defensive position was ideal. The approaching Mexican soldados were easily visible advancing toward the Texans's position behind a small enbankment. The enbankment allowed the Texans to partially show themselves, pick a target, fire, scamble down to safely reload their musket, then repeat the process again and again.

Rifleman Noah Smithwick described the ensuing carnage. "Our long rifles—and I thought I never heard rifles crack so keen, after the roar of the (Mexican) cannon-—mowed down the Mexicans at a rate that might well have made braver hearts . . . recoil. Three times they charged, but there was a platoon ready to receive them. Three times we picked off their gunners, the last one with a lighted match in his hand; then a panic seized them, and they broke. They jumped on the mules attached to the cannon, two or three to a mule, without even taking time to cut them loose, and struck out for the fort, leaving the loaded gun on the field. With a ringing cheer we mounted the bank and gave chase. We turned their cannon on them, adding wings to their flight. They dropped their muskets, and splashing through the shallow water of the river, fled helter skelter as if pursued by all the furies."[6]

The initial attack failed due to the accuracy of musket fire from the insurgents but the Mexicans tried three more times before retiring back to San Antonio. Mexican losses were ten dead and the abandoned six pound cannon. One insurgent (Richard Andrews) was mortally wounded and another injured. Bexarenos in town reported that the actual Mexican losses were seventy-five killed and wounded.[7]

Other reports indicate that General Cos was not physically present but had ordered Colonel Domingo Ugartechea to lead the 275 soldiers against the rebels.

The battle of Conception lasted only about thirty minutes. At its conclusion, the rest of the Texas army under General Austin was arriving from Mission Espada to establish his headquarters at Mission Concepcion.

The relative ease of the victory at Concepcion may have falsely encouraged Captain, later Colonel, James Fannin about his military prowess. Fannin had entered the United States Military Academy in 1819 but left in 1821. At the time of his departure, Fannin's academic standing was 60 of 86. Later, he was badly defeated by General Jose Urrea at Coleto Creek near Goliad and surrendered his entire force which was later massacred by order of Santa Anna.

Battlefield intelligence was seldom infallible. In November Texans learned the Mexicans were preparing a pack train to re-supply its encircled garrison in San Antonio. It was rumored that the pack train contained a silver payroll for the Mexican troops. Lieutenant Salvador Flores was ordered by Seguin to intercept the train and its supposed payroll on November 26. Instead of silver, Flores found the train was carrying hay. Flores' mission was at least a partial success in that many horses and mules were captured for use by Austin's force, as well as the hay. The encounter was dubbed the Grass or Zacate fight.[8]

Seventeen Mexican soldiers were killed or wounded at the Zacate fight. Flores' losses were four wounded.

Another Flores' assignment, that of burning hay and grass along the Mexican army's path to San Antonio, was so successful that Mexican cavalrymen in Santa Anna's advance element had to carry their saddles since no forage was available for their hungry mounts.

While Austin was besieging and planning to assault San Antonio, he called for local elections in Goliad and Victoria to select representatives to the Consultation initially suggested by Zavala and Seguin. Selectees included Placido Benavides, Juan Antonio Padilla and Sylvestre de Leon, all representing Victoria. The Consultation finally achieved a quorum on November 3, 1835. Several Tejanos attended one or more of the meetings. Among them were de Leon and Padilla, Benjamin Fulqua representing Austin's colony as well as Lorenzo de Zavala from Harrisburg. Zavala was especially active, helping draft a declaration of causes and a blueprint for a provisional government.

Some of the Consultation's fifty-eight delegates favored independence from the Mexican federation while others, including Zavala, preferred Texas remain a state within that federation. He wrote of the conflict "I sustained with heat the principles of the federal Mexican Constitution of 1824 (of which he was an author), and adhesion to Mexico upon this basis."[9]

After debate the delegates voted 33-15 to adopt a "Declaration of the People of Texas." The declaration affirmed their desire to support and uphold the Mexican Constitution of 1824, rejecting independence and remaining within the Mexican federation but as a separate (from Coahuila) state.

The Consultation also established a provisional government, a portion of which was a general council made up of a representative from each Texas municipality. Juan Padilla was one of the thirty-nine members of the council.

Three Tejanos, Benavides, Carbajal and Cuellar, were appointed regular army officers by the council.

Tejano Jose Cassiano, who married the daughter of Jose Antonio Menchaca, was a successful San Antonio merchant. During late 1835, Cassiano, an early advocate of Texas independence, generously made his store a supply point for the Texas army. Along with Blas Herrera, he also provided invaluable scouting reports on the whereabouts of Santa Anna's approaching army.

By the time operations against San Antonio de Bexar began December 5, 1835, the company of Captain Seguin numbered 65 men. However the official roster provided by the Commissioner of

Claims office contains 58 names, including Seguin, commanding officer; Placido Venavides (sic), first lieutenant; Salvador Flores, second lieutenant; and Manuel Flores, sergeant. The exact 1858 roster, containing original spellings, is at appendix B.

Erastus "Deaf" Smith, famous scout and long time resident of San Antonio, recommended the first insurgent objectives in taking the town from Mexican General Cos. Thick-walled houses on the north side of San Antonio were chosen for Ben Milam's initial attack. The houses were near the home of Gregorio Esparza, a member of Placido Benavides' Tejano company. Esparza took the opportunity to check on the welfare of his wife and children.

The next objective was the house of a Santa Anna adherent, Father de la Garza. Jose Domingo Losoya, also of Benavides' unit, was among those Tejanos wresting this tactically important location from its stubborn Mexican defenders. The de la Garza residence commanded good fields of fire toward the main plaza, as did the nearby Veramendi home of Jim Bowie's in-law family.

Milam instructed his men to avoid exposing themselves to Mexican fire by burrowing through the walls of the neighborhood. Once a wall was breached, the insurgents fought and clawed their way into the adjoining room. Their advance was slow but safer than exposing themselves to Cos' cannon fire in the open streets.

Milam scribbled a situation report to be sent to the anxious interim government assembling in San Felipe about the bravery of his Tejano-Texian troops. "They have so far had a fierce contest, the enemy offering a strong and obstinate resistance. It is difficult to determine what injury has been done him (General Cos), many killed, certainly, but how many cannot be told, On our side, ten or twelve wounded, two killed."

Tejanos living in San Antonio de Bexar facilitated communications between Austin and his scattered encircling army. Bexarenos even collected and returned spent cannon balls which Austin's artillery had fired at General Cos' soldiers.

Popular Colonel Ben Milam was killed by a Mexican sharpshooter as he stood in the courtyard of the Veramendi residence. Immediately the position of the shooter in a tree near the river was given away by his musket's report and he was dispatched by several of Milam's men. Milam was buried on the spot.

Milam was among the four insurgents killed at the battle of Bexar. There also were twenty to twenty-five wounded including valuable scout Erastus "Deaf" Smith.

Edward Burleson replaced Austin as the commanding general when Austin resigned from the Texas army and left to became Texas' commissioner to the United States. While in command, Austin attempted to convince as many members of Cos' soldiers as possible to desert in support of federalism and the Constitution of 1824. One such soldier, Jesus Cuellar, reported to Burleson that the Mexican soldiers' morale was so low that another Texas attack upon the town would be successful.

Dr. Joseph E. Field, who fought at both Bexar and Goliad, described the intensity of the fight inside San Antonio. "With crow bars we perforated the walls of the houses toward the square, making port holes, through which we kept up a constant fire at them . . . . In this way, and in opening communications with each other by means of ditches, we spent the day, the besieged keeping up a raking fire through the streets by day and by night."[10]

General Burleson ordered his approximately three hundred troops to resume the attack on December 9, 1835. Their assault consisted of a house-by-house, street-by-street struggle. Among the Tejanos participating in this successful attack were the companies of Placido Benavides and Juan Seguin. Among Seguin's volunteers were Ambrosio Rodriguez, Eduardo Ramirez, Pedro Herrera, Salvador Flores, Manuel Flores, Simon Arreola, Caesario Carmona, Vicente Zepeda, Jose Maria Arocha, (first name unknown) Silvero, Matias Curvier, Antonio Fuentes and Juan Antonio Badillo.

Benavides' company, part of the assaulting Second Division, encountered particularly heavy resistance from Cos' soldiers. General Austin praised Benavide's gallantry during the capture of the critically situated home of Juan M. Veramendi, the same house where Ben Milam was killed by a sniper. This home was the same that newly-arrived empresario Stephen F. Austin had visited in 1821.

Among the other volunteers was a famous company from outside Texas, the New Orleans Greys, who later defended the Alamo in company with many Tejanos and other volunteers. The flag of the New Orleans Greys was flown over the Alamo by the insurgents and is occasionally displayed at the Chapultepec museum in Mexico City. The myth that the Mexican flag emblazoned with 1824 (for the Constitution of 1824) was flown over the Alamo by its defenders cannot be confirmed. On the arrival of Santa Anna's advance guard, a flag depicting the State of Coahuila y Tejas was briefly observed by the Mexicans.

One brave Tejana, name unknown, filled two buckets of water from the river to carry to the thirsty insurgents. Mexican troops fired at her, killing her instantly.

Another Tejana, Maria Jesus de Garcia, was cited for rending "extraordinary" service to the Texas army by attempting to carry water to the Texans. She was shot and severely wounded by a centralista platoon firing from the Alamo. Even her water bucket was hit.[11]

After four days of unorthodox warfare General Cos lost some three hundred men while the insurgents thirty-five killed and wounded. Other researchers cite different losses for Cos. "In total, Cos appears to have suffered about 170 dead and wounded during the siege and storming of Bexar. He retreated from the city with over forty wounded men and left about fourteen men behind in the Alamo."[12]

Following the surrender of Cos on December 9, Captain Seguin and his company shadowed the retreating Cos force to the Rio Grande, protecting Texans and their property from deprivations by the defeated Mexican troops. Cos had surrendered, agreeing never to oppose constitutional government and was allowed to march his remaining troops out of Texas. Cos also pledged that he and his officers "would not in any manner oppose the reestablishment of the Federal Constitution of 1824."[13]

Seguin's ability and loyalty were recognized again when he, along with an artillery battery commanded by Lieutenant Colonel James C. Neill, were given responsibility for the defense of the town.

Seguin was also elected a town judge. In this role, he was instrumental in aiding two Tejanos, Jose Francisco Ruiz and Jose Antonio Navarro, travel to the Convention which produced the Texas Declaration of Independence.

In addition to Ruiz and Navarro, the citizens of Bexar elected Gaspar Flores to attend the March 1, 1836 Convention at Washington-on-the-Brazos where the Texas Declaration of Independence was drafted on March 2 and signed on March 3. Flores, several times alcalde of Bexar, did not attend since he was assisting his ailing friend Erasmo Seguin and family depart the town.

Seven Tejanos were elected to represent their constituencies at the 1836 Convention at Washington-on-the-Brazos. In addition to the above (Ruiz, Navarro and Gaspar Flores) they were Jose Maria Jesus Carbajal and Juan Antonio Padilla from Victoria, Erasmo Seguin of Bexar, and Lorenzo de Zavala of Harrisburg. Carbajal, fearing for the safety of his family, did not go to the Convention. Padilla attempted to attend but swollen rivers prevented his attendance. Erasmo Seguin, knowing his name was on Santa Anna's reprisal list, led his family and livestock to the east, out of danger.

Seguin's men continued to forage for food, supplies and provisions from nearby ranches to support the growing numbers of troops gathering at the Alamo.

Apparently Cos' defeat was not a surprise to Santa Anna. One of his officers wrote "General Cos had been hemmed in at Bejar, 480 leagues from the capital and in need of munitions and foodstuffs: desperate because he never received the help so frequently offered, he was compelled to capitulate on the 10th of December 1835."[14]

The companies of Seguin and Travis also cooperated in capturing a Mexican herd of two hundred horses on the Laredo road.

Later that month Mexican Minister of Defense and Marine Jose Maria de Tornel issued an ominous decree that Santa Anna would use as justification for his treatment of prisoners. The circular stated, in part:

"1st. All foreigners who disembark in any port of the Republic, or enter it by land, in arms, and with the object of attacking our territory, shall be treated and punished as pirates, in consideration of their not belonging to any nation with which the Republic is at war, and of their not following any recognized flag.

2nd. All foreigners who may disembark in any port or introduce by land arms and munitions of war destined for any district in revolt against the National Government, with the known object of placing such means of warfare in the hands of the enemy, shall be treated and punished in the same manners."

On April 6, 1836 a law was passed in Mexico City making the above even plainer. The punishment of prisoners of war captured in Texas would be death.

PLACIDO BENAVIDES MONUMENT IN VICTORIA, TEXAS
One portion of the inscription: "During Benavides'
leadership, a serious confrontation with Centralist troops
attempting to arrest his brother-in-law, Jose Maria
Carbajal, was peacefully avoided. Benavides responded to
the June, 1835 arrest order with the statement that he was
'a constitutional officer, and not at all amenable to the
military' of Santa Anna. Benavides' service during the
struggle to restore the Constitution of 1824 was
extraordinary. Ironically, however, he died during exile in
Opelousas, Louisiana, in 1837."
(photo courtesy of N. K. Rogers)

CHAPTER FIVE
TENSIONS AT GOLIAD AND GATHERING OF TROOPS AT THE ALAMO

Captain Philip Dimitt, in temporary command at the La Bahia presidio, had without consulting his provisional government issued a "Goliad Declaration of Independence" on December 20. This declaration of Texas independence flew in the face of what Zavala and the Consultation had agreed about Texas remaining in the Mexican federation but as a state separate from Coahuila.

Dimitt's declaration resolved that Texas should be a "free, sovereign and independent State." It contained ninety-one signatures including those of Tejanos Jose Miguel Aldrete and Jose Maria Jesus Carbajal. It preceded the more famous Texas Declaration of Independence issued by the provisional government by seventy-two days

A portion of Dimitt's document was offensive to many Tejanos because it degraded their contributions during the assault on Bexar. It also claimed that, based upon the insurgents' occupation of Goliad, some Tejanos remained attached to the "institutions of their ancient tyrants."[1]

Earlier, Governor of Coahuila y Tejas Augustin Viesca visited Goliad. Dimitt refused to recognize Viesca's position as governor, adding to Tejano anger. Dimitt considered the decision to recognize Viesca was that of the provisional government, not his.

Dimitt's actions caused many Tejanos to reexamine their loyalties to Texas. Some decided to side with the centralists instead.

Lieutenant Colonel James C. Neill and his engineering officer, Mr. Green B. Jameson, were busily improving the phyisical defenses of the Alamo. Walls were strengthened, catwalks within them erected and firing positions sandbagged. A total of twenty-one artillery pieces were collected, sited and installed within the old mission, one of which may have been the famous Gonzales "Come and Take It" cannon. The heaviest cannon, an eighteen-pounder, had been landed at Velasco with the volunteer company of New Orleans Greys. Unfortunately the basic load of powder and shot had not arrived on the same schooner with the Greys, the *Columbus.*

Tejano Damacio Ximenes, who fought beside Travis at Anahuac, the first battle of the revolution, helped manhandle the big cannon within the Alamo when he reentered the mission in March with Davy Crockett. Canoneer Ximenes' duty was to service the eighteen-pounder newly positioned on the Alamo's southwest corner. He probably fired the big cannon at Travis' order plainly replying in the negative to Santa Anna's demand for surrender.

According to Seguin, he was again commissioned on January 2, 1836, this time as a captain of "regular" cavalry. Salvador Flores received his captain's commission on January 14 while serving in the Alamo under Lieutenant Colonel James C. Neill. Captain Flores volunteered to scout the Mexican army's dispositions and plans in the Laredo area since rumors about a troop buildup to invade Texas were legion.

Colonel James Bowie joined Neill's force in the Alamo on January 19, 1836. Bowie, famous for his exploits and fighting knife, first settled in San Antonio in 1828. He became a Roman Catholic, a Mexican citizen and married a daughter of the rich and powerful Veramendi family. His wife, the nineteen year old, blonde Maria Ursula de Veramendi, later bore him two children. While on an 1833 business trip to Mississippi Bowie received the tragic news that his wife and several of her family had died from cholera in Monclova, Mexico, where they had been taken by Bowie to avoid the epidemic. A despondent Bowie returned to San Antonio, living with his two sisters-in-law at the Veramendi home.

Jose Cassiano, a wealthy San Antonio merchant and republican advocate of liberty, brought Neill the disquieting news that Santa Anna had arrived in Saltillo, Mexico on January 27 on his way north. Santa Anna was reported to have 3000 troops with him and General

Ramirez y Sesma at Rio Grande City, another 1600. Neill forwarded the information to General Houston, then at Goliad, then passed command of the Alamo and its troops to Colonel William B. Travis.

On February 10, Davy Crockett was welcomed to the Alamo with a party. During the party a messenger from Placido Benavides' company brought Travis news of a buildup of Mexican troops at Presidio Rio Grande preparing to march on Bexar. Not overly concerned with the news, Travis continued the party, remarking that it would take the Mexicans another thirteen days to arrive.

One criticism of Travis and Bowie is that they should have better utilized the scouting abilities of Captain Seguin's mounted company of volunteer Tejanos. So familiar were Seguin and his riders with the South Texas countryside that they could patrol even south of the Rio Grande River, providing invaluable information on Santa Anna's movements and activities.

Bits of intelligence about Mexican troop movements began filtering into the Alamo. On February 16 Ambrosio Rodriguez heard from his wife's cousin in Laredo about troop assemblies, which information was repeated to Travis on February 18. On the 20th one of Seguin's soldiers, his cousin Blas Herrera, riding with Jose Cassiano, reported seeing Santa Anna and an resplendent army estimated at 6,000 crossing the Rio Grande.

Apparently Travis took the last warning seriously since he convened a council of his officers that same night at 9:00. But the upshot of the meetings was that the stories were exaggerated and that Santa Anna's imminent arrival could not be true.

On his way into Texas, General Santa Anna met the just-defeated force of General Cos and ordered Cos to turn his troops around. Thus Cos and his officers violated their surrender agreement with General Burleson at Bexar. By this time, late February, Santa Anna's force totaled about four thousand. General Eugenio Tolza with another two thousand troops was enroute to join his general-in-chief.

On February 17, at the Nueces River, Santa Anna sent the following spirited message to his "army of operations" outlining its mission and patriotic purpose against the insurgent "wretches".

"COMPANIONS IN ARMS! Our most sacred duties have conducted us to these plains and urge us forward to combat with that mob of ungrateful adventurers on whom our authorities have incautiously lavished favors which they have failed to bestow on Mexicans. They have appropriated to themselves our territories, and have raised the standard of rebellion, in order that this fertile and expanded department may be detached from our Republic; persuading themselves that our unfortunate dissentions have incapacitated us for the defense of our native land. Wretches! They will soon see their folly.

SOLDIERS! Your comrades have been treacherously sacrificed at Anahuac, Goliad, and Bejar; and you are the men chosen to chastise the assassins.

MY FRIENDS! We will march to the spot whither we are called by the interests of the nation in whose services we are engaged. The candidates for "acres" of land in Texas will learn to their sorrow, that their auxiliaries from New Orleans, Mobile, Boston, New York, and other northern ports (from whence no aid ought to proceed) are insignificant, and that the Mexicans, though naturally generous, will not suffer outrages with impunity—injurious and dishonorable to their country—let the perpetrators be whom they may."
(signed) ANTONIO LOPEZ DE SANTA ANNA

Although he erred on the date of Santa Anna's arrival in San Antonio, Seguin wrote "On the 22d of February, at 2 P.M., General Santa Anna with over four thousand men took possession of the city. In the meantime, we fell back into the Alamo.

"On the 28th the enemy commenced the bombardment while we met in a council of war. . . . A majority of the council resolved that I should leave the fort and proceed with a communication to Colonel James W. Fannin, requesting him to come to our assistance."[2]

Santa Anna's actual arrival in San Antonio was February 23. He established his headquarters near the San Fernando church and ran up the ominous red flag, meaning "no quarter" for prisoners. Travis referred to Santa Anna as that "monster fighting us under a blood-red flag, threatening to murder all prisoners and make Texas a waste desert."

In addition to the red flag raised over the church signifying "no quarter" Santa Anna had issued the following standing order to his army.

"Now, this is very important and is to be stressed in any pronouncement we make. Any foreigner in Tejas who is arrested while in the possession of arms of any kind is to be judged a pirate and treated accordingly. Finally . . . once the battle begins, if the enemy has not previously surrendered, no prisoners will be taken. They are to be shot on the battlefield where we capture them."

One of the sergeants in Santa Anna's army was Francisco Becerra of the Matamoros Battalion. Becerra participated in the assault on the Alamo, later was taken prisoner at San Jacinto. For several years he lived in Texas, employed by R.M. Fuller who wrote "The Fall of the Alamo," the first of the Alamo chronicles published in 1860 by San Antonio's Herald Steam Press. Fuller's small, sixteen page pamphlet was based on interviews with Becerra, two other Mexican sergeants and General Thomas J. Rusk, former Texas secretary of war.

Becerra related a revealing incident concerning his general-in-chief's dalliance during the middle of an important campaign.

While searching for timbers to be used in building a bridge for the assault on the Alamo, General Manuel Castrillon entered a house, finding a lady and her beautiful daughter. Castrillon told Santa Anna about the meeting and Santa Anna "was in a great fever" to see the daughter. He commanded that the lady and daughter be taken to his quarters. General Minon complied, first delivering Santa Anna's message to the mother. She replied that she was a respectable lady, of good family, and had always conducted herself with propriety. She was the widow of an honorable man who had commanded a company in the service of Mexico. Santa Anna was not her president and couldn't get her daughter except by marriage.

General Minon reported the conversation to Santa Anna, adding that Minon had in his command a man, well-educated, yet rascally and capable of performing tricks, including impersonating a priest. The actor-pseudo-priest consented to solemnize the wedding between the young lady and Santa Anna in the latter's quarters. The "wedding" took place in late February. Later the "deceived and trusting young lady was sent to San Luis Potosi in the carriage of General Minon. . . . I do not know when she ascertained that Gen. Santa Anna was already a married man, and the father of a family, and that she had been made a victim of a foul and rascally plot."[3]

Accompanying many of the Alamo defenders, particularly the Tejanos, were their families coming into the old mission for protection against the centralistas. Among them was Gregorio Esparza's wife,

Ana Salazar de Esparza and her four children. One of them, Enrique, remembered other women taking refuge in the Alamo. Among them was Juana Losoya Melton, wife of Eliel Melton; Concepcion Losoya, Juana's mother and her sons Juan and Toribio; Vitorina de Salina and three girls; Trinidad Saucedo and Petra Gonzalez.

Enrique mentioned another woman known as Madame Candeleria who claimed to have nursed the ill Jim Bowie but whose presence in the Alamo has never been verified. She was the famous—living to a reported 113 years—wife of Candelario Villanueva, one of Seguin's men gathering at the Alamo. Seguin, remembering he had failed to lock the door of his San Antonio house, sent Villanueva to do so. By the time Villanueva had locked up, he could not get through the Mexican positions already encircling the old mission.

All the Tejanos in the Alamo could have escaped from the old mission and quickly disappeared into the darkened streets of San Antonio had it not been for their loyalty and devotion to the insurgents' cause. When questioned by Jim Bowie if he wanted to leave, cannoneer Gregorio Esparza replied "No, I will stay and die fighting."[4]

In later years Enrique Esparza, Gregorio's son, recalled that Santa Anna called a three-day truce during which a number of Tejanos left the Alamo. Enrique remembered incomplete names in most instances. They were the woman, Trinidad Saucedo; (no first name but possibly Antonio) Menchaca; (no first name) Flores; Rodriguez (no first name given but probably Guadalupe Rodriquez who entered the Alamo with Crockett); (no first name) Ramirez; (no first name) Arocha and (no first name) Silvero.

Santa Anna, his headquarters on La Plaza de Las Islas Street, settled down to reduce the Alamo's defenses with his cannon. He was reportedly incensed when he was almost killed by a long-range musket shot from Davy Crockett on the parapet of the Alamo. Santa Anna was so angered that he swore to assault the old mission the very next day.

The residents of San Antonio de Bexar found themselves again under a centralista army, this one under the command of the President of Mexico and General-in-Chief, Santa Anna. Some Bexarenos cooperated willingly with their new rulers. Others cooperated less willingly, their sympathies remaining with the insurgents now besieged in the crumbling Alamo. Many others, like acting alcalde Francisco Antonio Ruiz, son of Francisco Ruiz, chose to obey the current occupying force, whatever it represented. Ruiz, probably placed under house arrest by Santa Anna, later was ordered to identify the bodies of the more famous Alamo defenders like Bowie, Crockett and Travis. Ruiz also supervised the construction of the funeral pyre for the fallen defenders of the Alamo.

Seguin and Corporal Antonio Cruz y Arocha (also known as Antonio Cruz) escaped through the encircling Mexican lines on the night of February 29 to carry Travis' request for assistance to Fannin at Goliad. Earlier Seguin had gone to his bedridden good friend, Bowie, and asked to use Bowie's horse for this mission because Seguin's horse was lame. Bowie assented. It was the last time the two friends would see each other.

Travis message to Fannin warned "it will be impossible for us to keep them (the Mexican troops) out much longer." Travis dispatched another messenger, Alejandro de la Garza, to the provisional government with a similar plea for assistance.

Seguin and Cruz cautiously trotted their horses, avoiding the escape azimuths where they heard periodic shouts of "centinela alerta!" Once they were challenged but spurred their horses after a few words of explanation to a sleepy sentinel who fired at the sound of their galloping away.

After riding all night and escaping Mexican patrols Seguin and Antonio Cruz met Captain Francis L. Desauque of Fannin's command at the Cibolo Creek. Seguin knew Desauque because he had previously foraged on Seguin's ranch, taking cattle, corn and other provisions.

Desauque told Seguin that Fannin was already enroute to the Cibolo, thence to the Alamo to provide reinforcements to the besieged Travis and should arrive within two days. Seguin waited at the Cibolo while also transmitting Travis' plea for assistance to Fannin whom he believed to be on the march.

Fannin responded to Seguin, via a Lieutenant Charles Finley, saying he had advanced as far as Rancho Nuevo, some two miles west of Goliad on the San Antonio River. Fannin said there he had received news of the advance of Mexican General Jose Urrea and was forced to countermarch back to Goliad to defend it. Fannin advised Seguin to continue to Gonzales and deliver Travis' plea to General Houston.

Colonel Crockett and his scouts found a large group of volunteers on the Cibolo and led them into the Alamo, probably after midnight on March 4. Among the fifty or so volunteers were at least five men of Juan Seguin's company. They were Juan Abamillo, Juan A. Badillo, Carlos Espalier, Andres Nava, Guadalupe Rodriquez and cannoneer Damacio Ximenes.

There is evidence, remembered by Mexican General Vicente Filisola, that Travis offered to surrender on the evening of March 5 not realizing that Santa Anna just had finalized his plan to assault the Alamo early the next morning. If true, this validates Pena's recollection that Travis promised his men to either escape or surrender if no help had been received by March 5.

Angel Navarro of San Antonio crossed the river and approached the besieging Mexicans, asking that his relatives Juana Navarro Alsbury and Gertrudis Navarro be allowed to leave. Mrs. Alsbury was the wife of Dr. Horatio "Horace" Alsbury, who was away, warning Houston at Gonzales of the Alamo's desperate situation.

Mrs Alsbury relayed to Santa Anna or one of his staff that Travis would surrender his command if the lives of all the defenders would be spared. Santa Anna's reply was that Travis must surrender unconditionally, that traitors would receive no guarantees. The brave Mrs. Alsbury returned to the Alamo with this ominous answer.

Travis' plea for assistance did not fall on deaf ears in Gonzales where the Gonzales Ranging Company of twenty-two volunteers was preparing to go to the Alamo. After waiting impatiently for Fannin's command from Goliad, which never arrived, the Gonzales force hit the road for Bexar, adding more volunteers along the way.

By the time the relief force reached the Cibolo Creek near San Antonio on February 28, the volunteers numbered thirty-two. On the evening of February 29, they mounted their horses for the final eighteen-mile trek to the Alamo. Eventually following the bed of the San Antonio River for some distance, they covered the remaining three to four hundred yards of open terrain by a charge at the Alamo's gates. Fortunately, they were not detected or fired upon by the numerous nearby Mexican encampments. One of the "Gonzales thirty-two" was wounded in the foot by a musket shot from within the Alamo during their charge.

By three a.m. March 1 the Gonzales volunteers were reining up within the Alamo where they were greeted loudly and warmly for several hours that early morning. Among them was sixteen year old Tejano Galba Fuqua. With them, Fuqua later gave his life defending the Alamo.

Running out of food and water in the Alamo, Travis was urged by many of his men to either break out or consider surrendering to Santa Anna. Pressed for an answer, "on the 5th he promised them that if no help arrived on that day they would surrender or try to escape." Lieutenant Colonel Jose Enrique de la Pena, one of Santa Anna's officers at the Alamo, continued. "It was said as a fact during these days that the president-general had known of Travis's decision, and that it was for this reason that he precipitated the assault because he wanted to cause a sensation and would have regretted taking the Alamo without clamor and without bloodshed, for some believed that without these there is no glory."[5]

Rather than wait for the Travis to be starved out and capitulate, Santa Anna preferred to order the assault for "glory." The officer, Pena, criticized his commander further, observing "The Alamo was an irregular fortification without flank fires which a wiser general would have taken with insignificant losses, but we lost more than three hundred brave men."[6]

Some historians doubt that Pena's later memoirs—as opposed to his campaign diary—written while he was imprisoned in Mexico are authentic.

The attack plan called for four assaulting columns. Attacking the Alamo's northwest wall was General Perfecto de Cos (who previously surrendered at Bexar and been paroled, promising never to oppose constitutional government) leading the Aldama battalion and three companies from San Luis.

The second column, commanded by Colonel Duque, consisted of one battalion and three companies from San Luis attacking the north wall. Columns one and two totaled seven hundred men.

The third column, under Colonel Romero, had two companies of fusiliers (riflemen) from the Matamoros and Jimenez battalions with which to attack the eastern side, considered the best defended. This column had 300 men.

Column four under Colonel Morales contained over one hundred chasseurs (light cavalry) whose initial goal was the Alamo's entrance and its entrenchments.

Santa Anna's reserve, commanded by Colonel Amat, contained a zapadore (pioneer) battalion and five companies of grenadiers for a total of 400 men.

The total attacking force of Santa Anna was 1500 men, per Pena.

MARKER CITING THE FOUR REVOLUTIONARY FLORES
This Texas Historical marker memorializes early settler
Flores de Abrego. His descendants, Captain Salvador Flores,
Captain Manuel Flores, Lieutenant Nepomuceno Flores and
Private Jose Maria Flores all fought for Texas liberty. The
marker is in Floresville, Texas, named for their family.
(photo courtesy of N.K. Rogers)

CHAPTER SIX
THE ALAMO ASSAULT AND AFTERMATH

Since there were no surviving defenders of the Alamo, the only eye witnesses were the Mexicans themselves. One Mexican noncommissioned officer, Francisco Bercerra, took part in the assault by the third column, later wrote a book about his experiences. Dan Kilgore, introducing Becerra's book "A Mexican Sergeant's Recollections of the Alamo and San Jacinto" claims "More details of specific incidents during the bitter struggle derive from Becerra than from any other participant."[1]

"On the morning of March 6, 1836 at four o'clock, the bugle sounded the advance," Becerra wrote. "The troops under Gen. Castrillon (assumed command upon Colonel Duque's death) moved in silence. They reached the fort, planted scaling-ladders, and commenced ascending; some mounted on the shoulders of others; a terrific live fire belched from the interior; men fell from the scaling-ladders by the score, many pierced through the head by balls, others fell by clubbed guns. The dead and the wounded covered the ground. After half an hour of fierce conflict, after the sacrifice of many lives, the column under Gen. Castrillon succeeded in making a lodgement in the upper part of the Alamo. It was a sort of outwork. I think it is now used as a lot, or as a courtyard. This seeming advantage was a mere prelude to the desperate struggle which ensued. The doors of the Alamo building were barricaded by bags of sand as high as the neck of a man, the windows also. On the top of the roofs of the different apartments were rows of sand bags to cover the besieged.

"Our troops, inspirited by success, continued the attack with energy and boldness. The Texians fought like devils. It was at short range—muzzle to muzzle—hand to hand—musket and rifle—bayonet and Bowie knife—all were mingled in confusion. Here a squad of Mexicans, there a Texian or two. The crash of firearms, the shouts of defiance, the cries of the dying and wounded, made a din almost infernal. The Texians defended desperately each inch of the fort—overpowered by numbers, they would be forced to abandon a room; they would rally in the next, and defend it until further resistance became impossible.

"Gen. Eugenio Tolza's command (the fourth column led by Colonel Morales) forced an entrance at the door of the church building. He met the same determined resistance without and within. He won by force of numbers, and at a great cost of life.

"There was a long room on the ground floor-it was darkened. Here the fight was bloody. It proved to be the hospital. The sick and the wounded fired from their beds and pallets. A detachment of which I had command had captured a piece of artillery. It was placed near the door of the hospital, doubly charged with grape and canister, and fired twice. We entered and found the corpses of fifteen Texians. On the outside we afterwards found forty-two dead Mexicans.

"On the top of the church building I saw eleven Texians. They had some small pieces of artillery and were firing on the cavalry, and those engaged in making the escalade. Their ammunition was exhausted, and they were loading with pieces of iron and nails. The captured piece was placed in a position to reach them, doubly charged, and fired with so much effect, that they ceased working their pieces.

"In the main building, on the ground floor, I saw a man lying on a bed-he was evidently sick. I retired without molesting him, notwithstanding the order of Gen. Santa Anna to give no quarter to the Texians. A sergeant of artillery entered before I had finally left the room-he leveled his piece at the prostrate man; the latter raised his hand and shot the sergeant through the head with a pistol. A soldier of the Toluca Regiment came in, aimed his gun at the invalid, and was killed in a similar manner. I then fired and killed the Texian. I took his two empty pistols, and found his rifle standing by his bed. It seemed he was too weak to use it.

"In another room I saw a man sitting on the floor among feathers. A bugler, who was with me, raised his gun. The gentleman said to him in Spanish:-'Don't kill me-I have plenty of money.' He pulled out a pocketbook, also a large roll of bank bills, and handed the latter to the bugler. We divided the money.

"While this was occurring another Texian made his appearance. He had been lying on the floor, as if resting. When he arose I asked:-'How many is there of you?' He replied:-'Only two.'

"The gentleman, who spoke Spanish, asked for Gen. Cos, and said that he would like to see him. Just then Gen. Amador came in. He asked why the orders of the President had not been executed, and the two Texians killed. In answer the bugler exhibited his roll of bank bills, and they were taken from him immediately by the general. In a few moments, Gen. Cos, Gen. Almonte, and Gen. Tolza, entered the room. As soon as Gen. Cos saw the gentleman who spoke Spanish he rushed to him, and embraced him. He told the other generals it was Travis, that on a former occasion he had treated him like a brother, had loaned him money, etc. He also said the other man was Col. Crockett. He entreated the other generals to go with him to Gen. Santa Anna, and join him in a request to save the lives of the two Texians. The generals and the Texians left together to find Santa Anna. The bugler and myself followed them. They encountered the commander-in-chief in the courtyard, with Gen. Castrillon. Gen. Cos said to him:-'Mr. President, you have here two prisoners—in the name of the Republic of Mexico I supplicate you to guarantee the lives of both.' Santa Anna was very much enraged. He said:-'Gentlemen generals, my order was to kill every man in the Alamo,' He turned and said:-'Soldiers, kill them.' A soldier was standing near Travis, and presented his gun at him. Travis seized the bayonet, and depressed the muzzle of the piece to the floor, and it was not fired. While this was taking place the soldiers standing around opened fire. A shot struck Travis in the back. He then stood erect, folding his arms, and looked calmly, unflinchingly, upon his assailants. He was finally killed by a ball passing through his neck. Crockett stood in a similar position. They died undaunted like heroes."[2]

The deaths of most heroes are told and re-told and the ensuing stories seldom agree. The death of Travis is an example. According to Alamo historian Walter Lord, Travis died on the north wall during the first assault.

Accompanied by his servant, Joe, Travis was armed with sword and shotgun and was encouraging some of Seguin's men. When scaling ladders appeared on the wall, Travis leaned over and fired his shotgun into the faces of the climbers. Immediately he was stuck in the head by a shot from below and rolled back onto an earthen embankment, near a cannon. There he sat, stunned and dying.[3]

Becerra continued his recollection of the encounter between Generals Cos and Santa Anna. "The firing was brisk for a time. It came from all sides. Gen. Santa Anna and most of the officers ran. Gen. Castrillon squatted down—so did I. In this affair eight Mexican soldiers were killed and wounded by their comrades.

"I did not know the names of the two Texians, only as given by Gen. Cos. The gentleman he called Crockett had on a coat with capes to it.

"The Alamo, as has been stated, was entered at daylight—the fighting did not cease till nine o'clock.

Gen. Santa Anna directed Col. Mora to send out his cavalry to bring in wood. He ordered that they should make prisoners of all inhabitants they might meet, and force them to pack wood to the Alamo. In this manner a large quantity of wood was collected. A large pile was raised. It consisted of layers of wood and layers of corpses of Texians. It was set on fire. The bodies of those brave men, who fell fighting that morning, as men have seldom fought, were reduced to ashes before the sun had set. It was a melancholy spectacle."[4]

Ana Salazar de Esparza's husband, Gregorio, was killed while manning his small cannon. His wife and children survived the bloodshed and later were allowed to leave. Her son, Enrique, witnessed the assault and later the incineration of the defenders' bodies. Enrique also remembered Mexican soldiers firing their muskets into the room where he hid, killing a young man near him. Then the soldiers ransacked the room, looking for valuables and money.

According to Walter Lord, "A minimum of ten Mexican women and children also survived: Mrs. Juana Alsbury and her baby; her sister Gertrudis Navarro; Mrs. Gregoria Esparza with her four children; Trinidad Saucedo and Petra Gonzales."[5]

Senora Andrea Castanon Villanueve, better known as Madame Candelaria, claimed to have been in the Alamo attending Jim Bowie. She was the wife of Candelario Villanueva who was dispatched by

Juan Seguin to lock the door of Seguin's house in San Antonio. Thus Candelario was unable to join Seguin and the others in the Alamo before its encirclement. During her long life of 113 years Madame Candelaria attracted many visitors to her home on South Laredo Street in San Antonio, recounting her experiences. However, her presence in the Alamo has never been verified.

Gregorio Esparza's body was found slumped beside his cannon. His brother, Francisco, approached General Cos and requested he be allowed to bury Gregorio. Since Francisco had fought under General Cos at Bexar, his wish to bury his brother was approved. Gregorio was the only Alamo defender to be buried, not burned.

Sergeant Becerra commented on the Mexican dead and their burial. "There was an order to gather our own dead and wounded. It was a fearful sight. Our lifeless soldiers covered the grounds surrounding the Alamo. They were heaped inside the fortress. Blood and brains covered the earth, and the floors, and had spattered the walls, The ghostly faces of our comrades met our gaze, and we removed them with despondent hearts. Our loss in front of the Alamo was represented as two thousand killed, and more than three hundred wounded. The killed were generally struck on the head. The wounds were in the neck and shoulder, seldom below that. The firing of the besieged was fearfully precise. When a Texas rifle was leveled on a Mexican he was considered as good as dead. All this indicates the dauntless bravery and the cool self-possession of the men who were engaged in a hopeless conflict with an enemy numbering more than twenty to one. They inflicted on us a loss ten times greater than they sustained. The victory of the Alamo was dearly bought. Indeed, the price in the end was well nigh the ruin of Mexico.

"During the evening we buried our dead. These were sad duties which each company performed for its fallen members."[6]

General Santa Anna, viewing the corpses of his dead soldiers following the Alamo victory, callously remarked "These are the chickens. Much blood has been shed; but the battle is over. It was but a small affair."[7]

Other historians have researched Mexican losses at the Alamo. "Nineteen sources give nineteen different answers—ranging from 65 killed and 223 wounded (Colonel Almonte) to 2000 killed and 300 wounded (Sergeant Becerra)" wrote Walter Lord. " . . . Best estimate seems to be about 600 killed and wounded. . . . Judging from Filisola's order of battle figures and Santa Anna's attack order of March 5, there were no more than 2400 Mexicans in San Antonio, or 1800 in the actual assault. (Note: The discrepancy between Lord's assaulting troop total of 1800 and Pena's 1500 is that Lord's included General Sesma's cavalry force of 300. Sesma's mission was to prevent Fannin from reinforcing the Alamo from Goliad) A casualty rate of 33 percent is a stiff price, even if 600 seems a modest figure."[8]

As to Texas losses at the Alamo, "Figures range from 180 to Santa Anna's ludicrous 600. Best estimate seems to be 183. This is the final figure given by Ramon Caro, the Mexican general's secretary."[9]

ASSAULT ON THE ALAMO: 4:00 a.m. MARCH 6, 1836

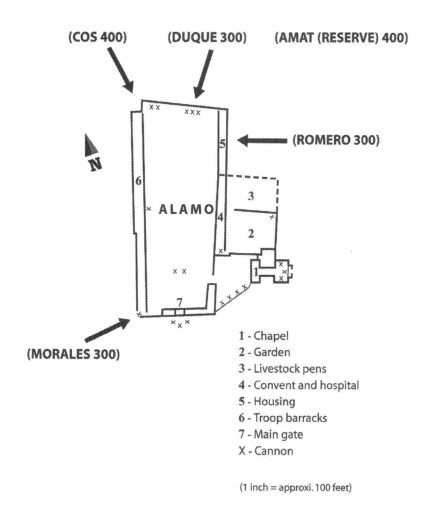

(COS 400)   (DUQUE 300)   (AMAT (RESERVE) 400)

(ROMERO 300)

N

ALAMO

(MORALES 300)

1 - Chapel
2 - Garden
3 - Livestock pens
4 - Convent and hospital
5 - Housing
6 - Troop barracks
7 - Main gate
X - Cannon

(1 inch = approxi. 100 feet)

Note: (Commander's Name and Troop Strengths) from Becerra's "Recollections"

CHAPTER SEVEN
TEJANO CASUALTIES AT THE ALAMO

On March 6, Seguin and his company rode toward Bexar with provisions for the Alamo. When they reached Cibolo Creek, they learned of the Alamo's fall by the silence of Travis' regular cannon signal meaning the Alamo still resisted. They returned to Gonzales to report the sad news to Houston.

Two of Seguin's men, Anselmo Bergara and Andreas Barcena, were detailed to remain in the San Antonio area to observe Mexican movements. They reported to Houston on March 11 that they heard that the Alamo had fallen and all its defenders killed. Fearing the effect of this demoralizing—perhaps doubtful—news on his army, Houston had the two Tejanos arrested and confined as spies.

Eight soldiers of the Seguin-Benavides companies were reported killed defending the old mission by historian Amelia W. Williams in her early work "A Critical Study of the Siege of the Alamo and of the Personnel of its Defenders." The eight were Juan Abanillo, Juan Antonio Badillo, Gregorio Esparza, Antonio Fuentes, Galba Fuqua, Jose Maria Guerrero, Domingo Losoyo and Andres Nava.[1]

Texas historian, Walter Lord, identifies seven Tejanos who died at the Alamo. Lord's list includes six from San Antonio: Juan Abamillo, Juan A. Badillo, Carlos Espalier, Gregorio Esparza, Antonio Fuentes, and Andres Nava. From Gonzales was Galba Fuqua.[2]

Historian Thomas Lloyd Miller studied land grant and other records, developing the following list of six—not seven or eight—Tejanos killed at the Alamo. His study also developed the following information concerning each individual.[3]

Private Juan Abamillo or Abanillo. Born and resided in San Antonio. No land grant cited.

Sergeant Juan Antonio Badillo. Resided in San Antonio. No land grant cited.

Private Gregorio Esparza, age 33. Born and resided in San Antonio. Took part in the siege and assault of Bexar, wresting it from Mexican General Cos. His heirs eventually received two land grants for his service. One was for 640 acres for his Alamo service. The other was for 1920 acres for service in the Texas army from November 1835 to March 1836 and for having fallen at the Alamo.

Private Antonio Fuentes. Native and resident of San Antonio, age 23. His heirs received 1920 acres for unspecified service.

Private Galba Fuqua. Age 16. Young Fuqua was one of the thirty-two volunteers from Gonzales who answered Travis' call for assistance. They succeeded in penetrating the Mexican positions encircling the Alamo, entered the mission and later died in its defense. Fuqua's heirs received 640 acres for his Alamo service. A second grant of 1920 acres was for service from February to March 1836, when he perished at the Alamo.

Private Andres Nava. Native and resident of San Antonio, age 26. Nava's heirs received no land grant because reportedly they were too poor to complete filing their claim.

Miller's research determined that the following two Tejanos, previously thought to have perished at the Alamo, did not.

Private Jose Maria Guerrero. Resident of Laredo, age 43. Often called Brigido Guerrero or "old, one-eyed Guerrero," he locked himself in a vacant cell, then convinced the Mexican soldiers capturing him that he had been a prisoner of the Texans, thus his life was spared.

Private Toribio Domingo Losoyo. Native and resident of San Antonio. Losoyo was a member of Juan Seguin's company during the siege of Bexar, for which his heirs received a land grant of 640 acres. Three legal instruments were found proving Losoyo did not die at the Alamo.

Although the two Tejanos mentioned above did not die in the Alamo, their services to Texas are equally valued.

A seventh Tejano killed in action at the Alamo was Private Carlos Espalier of Bexar. He served in the Benavides' company during the capture of Goliad and entered the Alamo sometime in February, then departed. He returned to the Alamo on approximately February 23. Espalier attended his friend, Jim Bowie on his sick bed and was killed during the March 6 assault on the mission.

Finally, in 1986 his descendants' petition for recognition of the Alamo service of Private Damacio Ximenes (also spelled Jimenez) was discovered in the Bexar County archives. Ximenes' name was added to the list of those Tejanos who gave their lives in defense of liberty at the Alamo. He was the only Tejano fighting under Travis at the first battle for Texas liberty at Anahuac. He was the eighth Tejano to date recognized for his ultimate sacrifice at the Alamo.

Designated later to pay honor to the fallen heroes of the Alamo was Lieutenant Colonel Juan Seguin. His March 13, 1837 letter to General Albert Sidney Johnston, then commander-in-chief of the Texas army, details those honors, Seguin's painstaking efforts and descriptions.

" . . . I caused the honors of war to be paid to the remains of the Heroes of Alamo on the 25th of Feby last. The ashes were found in three heaps. I caused a coffin to be prepared neatly covered with black, the ashes from the two smaller heaps were placed therein and with a view to attach additional solemnity to the occasion were carried to the Parish Church in Bexar whence it moved with the procession at 4 O'Clock on the afternoon of the day above mentioned. The Procession passed through the principal street of the city, crossed the River and passing through the principal avenue arrived at the spot whence part of the ashes had been collected, the procession halted, the coffin was placed upon the spot, and three volleys of musquetry were discharged over it by one of the companies, proceeding onward to the second spot from whence the ashes were taken where the same honors were done and thence to the principal spot and place of interment, the coffin was then placed upon the large heap of ashes when I addressed a few words to the Battallion and assemblage present in honor of the occasion in the Castillian language as I do not possess the English. Major Western then addressed the concourse in the latter tongue, the coffin and all the ashes were then interred and three volleys of musquetry was fired over the grave by the whole Battallion with an accuracy that would do honor to the best disciplined troops. We then marched back to quarter in the city with music and colors flying. Half hour guns were not fired because I had no powder for the purpose, but every honor was done within the reach of my scanty means. I hope as a whole my efforts may meet your approbation.

I have the honor to be
Very Respecty, yr obt. Sert.
John N. Seguin
Lieut. Col. Commg."

CHAPTER EIGHT
GENERAL URREA'S SUCCESSFUL SKIRMISHES AND THE CONVENTION MEETING AT WASHINGTON-ON-THE-BRAZOS

While Santa Anna was reducing the Alamo's thin fortifications with cannon, his best general, General of Brigade Jose Urrea, was smashing small groups of insurgents in the area south of Goliad.

General Urrea departed Matamoros February 18. According to Fuller, Urrea's force consisted of the Cuatla cavalry regiment (about 350 men), the Yucatan infantry battalion (another 350), and several companies of permanent militia. Fuller estimates Urrea's total complement as 900-1000 men.[1]

According to George O. Coalson, Urrea left Matamoros with only 350 men, which would have been only the Cuatla cavalry regiment. Urrea probably left his slow-moving infantry and militia behind as he galloped his cavalry to the insurgent positions located for him by centralist Tejanos loyal to Santa Anna.

Urrea's mission was to clear the coastal areas and eliminate the insurgents who might be planning on invading Mexico and capturing Matamoros behind Santa Anna's back. Receiving excellent intelligence from centralist-minded rancheros in South Texas, Urrea headed toward San Patricio, a small settlement some fifty miles south of Goliad.

The insurgents, headed by Francis W. Johnson and Doctor James Grant, were busily gathering horses from the countryside for use in the planned march toward Matamoros.

A herd gathered by Grant from southern ranches was driven to the ranch of Julian de la Garza. Johnson and twelve men were left at the Garza ranch to guard the horses. Later Johnson's force of twelve was increased by later arrivals from Doctor Grant's group.

General Urrea's diary entry reads as follows. "I arrived in San Patricio at three in the morning (February 27) and immediately ordered a party of thirty men headed by Captain Raphael Pretalia to proceed to the ranch of Don Julian de la Garza (a league distant) to attack the twelve or fifteen men who were guarding 150 horses there. I ordered forty dragoons of the remaining force to dismount; and dividing them into three groups under good officers, I gave instructions for them to charge the position of the enemy, protected by the rest of our mounted troops. The enemy was attacked at half past three in the morning in the midst of the rain, and although forty men within the fort defended themselves resolutely, the door was forced at dawn, sixteen being killed and twenty-four taken prisoners."[2]

Mexican Lieutenant Colonel Jose Enrique de la Pena's account of the victory details how Urrea surprised the insurgents after a difficult forced march in which six of his own soldiers died of exposure. "General Urrea was eager to meet with the enemy and, with the knowledge that the force marching toward Matamoros had countermarched toward San Patricio, he forced a march with part of the cavalry, leaving the infantry and convoy behind. On the 25th, 26th, and 27th of February, the soldiers were exposed to a severe storm, during which six from Yucatan, being from a tropical climate and unable to withstand the excessive cold, perished. Taking advantage of the bad weather and marching through forests and creeks, General Urrea was able to surprise the enemy at San Patricio at three o'clock in the morning, inflicting a loss of twenty dead and thirty-two prisoners, with no losses to himself other than one dragoon dead and four wounded.[3]

(Notes: The Texan casualty figures given above by Urrea are sixteen KIA and twenty-four prisoners while Pena cites twenty KIA and thirty-two POW. Most historians agree with Pena's figures of twenty insurgents killed and thirty-two prisoners. Apparently Urrea's six soldiers who died during the approach march were not of sufficient importance to Urrea to be considered losses.)

Among the insurgents killed at San Patricio, two were unnamed Tejanos from Bexar and two Americans from Grant's command. Of the prisoners captured at San Patricio and sent to Matamoros, four were Tejanos. The one named prisoner was Zambrano, the other three names were not recorded by Urrea.

Santa Anna apparently was dissatisfied with Urrea's report of his San Patricio victory. On March 3, three days before he was to inflict the same lethal punishment upon prisoners at the Alamo, he reminded Urrea of the Tornel decree requiring "That any foreigners invading the Republic be treated and tried as pirates whenever found armed." Santa Anna added any "Mexican who engages in the traitorous act of joining adventurers . . . loses his rights as citizen according to our laws . . ."[4]

On March 2, Urrea's cavalry located more insurgents at Agua Dulce creek, some 25 miles south of San Patricio. Some twenty-five insurgents, commanded by Dr. James Grant had been rounding up mounts for the Matamoros expedition, were ambushed and easily defeated. Twelve, including Grant, were killed. Six were captured and sent to Matamoros for imprisonment, including two Tejanos, one of who was named Cayetano. Six of Grant's small force escaped and joined Fannin.

Notable among the escapees was First Lieutenant Placido Benavides who commanded his own company during the war. Benavides warned Grant that more than sixty of Urrea's attacking dragoons had just cut the column between themselves and their horse herd. Benavides wanted to immediately engage the Mexicans but was ordered by Grant to escape and ride to Goliad to warn Fannin about Urrea's presence.

Benavides rode furiously to spread the word of Urrea's proximity. First he yelled warnings to the citizens of San Patricio then he rode onward to Refugio and Goliad, where he delivered the message to Fannin. Finally an exhausted rider and horse galloped into his own town of Victoria with the alarming news of Urrea's advance. For his warnings to citizens, Benavides is revered as the "Paul Revere of the Texas Revolution."

Pena's account of the Agua Dulce ambush provides more details. "On the first day of this month (March, 1836) General Urrea had news that Dr. James Grant was returning from Rio Bravo (the Rio Grande), where he had marched with a party of select riflemen in an exploratory excursion to round up horses, and during the night General Urrea started moving with eight dragoons to encounter him, but since the weather was so harsh and so excessively cold, it was necessary to await him at a point called Los Cuates de Agua Dulce. The next morning he dealt Grant a decisive blow; forty-two men were killed, including Grant and Major Morris; some prisoners, firearms, and horses in their possession were the fruits of the day's labor. . . . After he returned from the expedition against Grant, he stayed at San Patricio awaiting that part of his section which had remained in Matamoros and which joined him on the 7th."[5]

(Note: Pena's claim of forty-two men killed at Agua Dulce includes a number of Tejanos of the Benavides company who had joined the Grant contingent. As many as twenty-four Tejanos were killed at Agua Dulce, making it the most bloody revolutionary battle suffered by Tejanos. Doctor Grant's original party consisted of only 25, including him.)

A Tejano nicknamed "Comanche," Jesus Cuellar, bravely attempted to split Urrea's force so that Fannin might attack it in detail. Cuellar previously served under General Cos at Bexar but switched sides to be with the insurgents. From the diary of Mexican Colonel Francisco Garay: "On the night of the 7th (March) Jesus Cuellar, known as el Comanche, presented himself in San Patricio claiming that he had abandoned Fannin's force to throw himself upon the clemency of the Mexican Government. He was very likely sent by Fannin to observe our force and positions. He told General Urrea that Fannin had decided to attack him and that by this time he had probably effected a juncture with the force of the Mission Concepcion. He promised to take us to a spot where we could lay in ambush while he went and brought the enemy into our hands. . . . His brother, Salvador, who had accompanied our forces ever since we left Matamoros, pledged himself for his brother's loyalty. General Urrea, confiding in his sincerity, ordered 200 men, 1 cannon and 150 cavalry to set out early in the morning of the 8th of March for Las Ratas, 8 leagues away, on the San Refugio road. When our destination was reached, Cuellar left us and General Urrea proceeded to arrange the small force to carry out his plans. . . . The surprise would have been difficult in the location chosen, for the woods where we were to hide was extremely sparse and the trees were dry and devoid of foliage. . . . General Urrea must have realized our disadvantageous position for at midnight he ordered us to return to our camp."[6]

Tejano Cuellar's brave and ambitious ruse failed since he was unable to urge Colonel Fannin to attack although he convinced General Urrea to prepare an ambush.

In the midst of the bad news about the Santa Anna and Urrea military victories, Texas representatives were meeting at Washington-on-the-Brazos, near Brenham, to decide their political future.

The February 1 elections in Bexar resulted in four Tejanos chosen to attend the Convention. They were Jose Antonio Navarro, Juan Seguin, Miguel Arciniega and Jose Francisco Ruiz. Other reports indicate that Erasmo Seguin, Juan's father, was elected. Elected or not, an ailing Erasmo Seguin was busily gathering his family and as many sheep as he could collect and heading toward relative safety in East Texas. Victoria voters selected Jose Maria Jesus Carbajal to the Convention while those in Goliad sent Encarnacion Vasquez and, from Harrisburg rode Lorenzo de Zavala.

Not all the elected representatives were able to attend the Convention, some of them due to Urrea's successful advance. Among those unable to attend were Juan Seguin, at Gonzales with his Tejano company, and Arciniega. Also originally elected from Bexar was Gaspar Flores and, according to some historians, Erasmo Seguin, neither of whom attended the Convention.

Public opinion had previously supported the Constitution of 1824 and Texas becoming an independent state (not attached to Coahuila) within the Mexican federation. This had been reiterated as recently as the Consultation's declaration of November 1835. But by the time the Convention met in Washington-on-the-Brazos on March 1 1836 that opinion and delegate votes had gravitated for an independent Texas. "In the elections to the Convention, the independent candidate won a smashing victory in every Texas municipality."[7]

Friends of Jose Francisco Navarro said "he trembled at the thought of having to sanction with his signature (on the Texas Declaration of Independence) the eternal separation of Texas from the mother country." Nonetheless, Navarro and Ruiz, his uncle, participated in the convention and signed the document. Navarro also played a leading role in drafting the Texas Constitution.

Nor was it an easy decision for Lorenzo de Zavala. Although he had earlier wanted Texas to remain in the Mexican federation, hoping that liberal elements within Mexico would revolt against Santa Anna's excesses, he changed his mind about this possibility. On March 3, he, Navarro and Ruiz signed the Texas Declaration of Independence that had been drafted the previous day. Next came a constitution for the newly independent Republic of Texas adopted on March 15. Zavala was also on the committee drafting the new constitution. On March 17 Zavala was unanimously elected Vice President of the interim government of the Republic of Texas.

Pena's diatribe against these Tejanos was both scathing and allegorical. "This declaration (Texas Declaration of Independence) was also useful to the Mexicans, for, once they saw these incidents in proper perspective, they knew exactly where they stood. The cry of independence darkened the magic of liberty that had misled some of the less careful thinkers, and the few who had cast their lot with the colonists, believing them to be acting in good faith, disassociated themselves immediately, there remaining with the colonists only Don Lorenzo de Zavala, and the Bejar natives, Don Antonio Navarro and Don Juan Seguin, the only intelligent men who incurred the name of traitor, a label both ugly and deserved."[8]

The Convention's declaration drafted March 2, 1836, during Santa Anna's siege of the Alamo, listed a number of grievances against the government of Mexico.

Among the grievances were the following. "In this expectation (that Texans would continue to enjoy constitutional liberty and republican government) they have been cruelly disappointed, inasmuch as the Mexican nation has acquiesced in the late changes made in the government by General Antonio Lopez de Santa Anna, who, having overturned the constitution of his country, now offers us the cruel alternative, either to abandon our homes acquired by so many privations, or submit to the most intolerable of all tyranny, the combined despotism of the sword and the priesthood.

"It has sacrificed our welfare to the state of Coahuila, by which our interest have been continually depressed through a jealous and partial course of legislation, carried on at a far distant seat of government, by a hostile majority, in an unknown tongue, and this too, notwithstanding we have petitioned in the humblest terms for the establishment of a separate state government, and have, in accordance with the provisions of the national constitution, presented to the general Congress a republican constitution, which was, without just cause, contemptuously rejected."

The declaration concludes with the following. "We, therefore, the delegates with plenary powers of the people of Texas, in solemn convention assembled, appealing to a candid world for the necessities of our condition, do hereby resolve and declare, that our political connection with the Mexican nation has forever ended, and that the people of Texas do now constitute a free, Sovereign, and independent republic, and are fully invested with all the rights and attributes which properly belong to independent nations; and, conscious of the rectitude of our intentions, we fearlessly and confidently commit the issue to the decision of the Supreme arbiter of the destinies of nations."

The entire text of the declaration appears at Appendix C.

One of the Convention delegates hurriedly left Washington-on-the-Brazos for Gonzales to assemble the vestiges of an army to defend the new republic against a powerful and numerically superior enemy army already within its gates. The delegate was Sam Houston.

CHAPTER NINE
EYES ON GOLIAD

On March 10 Colonel James Fannin, the commander at Goliad/ La Bahia, sent Captain Amos B. King, twenty-eight men and much of Fannin's transport to help evacuate a family left behind at Refugio when they heard of the approach of General Urrea.

King and his men, described as "a company of infantry," arrived at Mission Refugio without enemy contact. Hearing of another distant family needing assistance, King divided his small company to send help to the second family.

On March 12 King was surprised by an armed group of South Texas rancheros led by Carlos de la Garza, the leading centralist Tejano of the area. Historians do not agree, as is often the case, upon the strength of the Garza force. Some said eighty, another "two hundred Mexican Ranchiers and Indians."[1]

While engaging Garza's force, King encountered an advance element of Urrea's cavalry and retreated to positions within the Mission Nuestra Senora del Rosario at Refugio. King immediately sent a rider to Fannin at Goliad asking for assistance.

Fannin dispatched Lieutenant Colonel Willliam Ward and the Georgia Battalion of 120 men to rescue King. Ward arrived at the mission at 3:00 p.m. on March 13 and succeeded in scattering the Mexicans besieging King. Rather than retreat back to Goliad to join Fannin, the two commanders, King and Ward, argued about which was in charge and split their forces. King, anxious to punish the centralist rancheros, took his men with some of Ward's in pursuit. King ambushed some of the ranchers, killing eight.

Meanwhile, Urrea, acting upon the excellent intelligence provided him by local rancheros, dispatched a cavalry company under Captain Rafael Pretalia to hold Ward's force at the mission for the slower arrival of Urrea and his infantry.

Urrea arrived at dawn on March 14, surrounded the mission and assaulted it three times with numerous losses. Inside, Ward's diminished force had few casualties but food, water and ammunition were running low. Another rider was sent to Fannin at Goliad asking for more assistance.

King and his men attempted to return to the besieged mission during the early afternoon but ran into Urrea's rear guard and took cover in a grove of trees next to the Mission River. King's sharpshooting riflemen inflicted numerous casualties on Urrea's soldiers.

Fannin's reply to Ward's request for assistance was to order Ward to fall back to Victoria, where Fannin had been ordered by Houston. Ward left volunteers with his wounded and the families on the night of the 14th. He chose an escape route toward Copano on the coast, trying to evade Urrea's cavalry patrols. During the night, King and his men also attempted to escape.

King's company crossed the Mission River that night but was discovered by locals who told Urrea of its location. When attempting to fight, King found most of his gunpowder was wet and useless due to the river crossing. The rancheros captured King and his men and marched them back to the mission.

There on March 16 King and his men were executed. Of King's command, thirty-five were killed in action or executed. Seven were captured but not killed. Among them was wounded Abraham H. Osborn, spared by General Urrea from execution due to the appeals of a Tejano named Cobian and his wife.[2]

Ward was able to evade capture during his flight to Victoria, only to find Victoria already occupied by Urrea. Some of Ward's insurgents made their way to Dimitt's Landing where, again, they found themselves facing Urrea's men and surrendered.

During its exhausting retreat, Ward's force was almost annihilated by Urrea's men and their ranchero allies.

Although records are incomplete, Ward's force, originally 120 men, suffered the following:[3]

Lost or escaped near Victoria on March 16: seven

Killed in action at Victoria on March 21: one

Prisoners executed near Victoria March 21: ten

Left at the Guadalupe River during the night of March 21 and later escaped: ten

Prisoners detailed to build boats at the Guadalupe River, March 23, and later escaped: sixteen

Captured at Victoria and interrogated by General Urrea, later escaped: five

Escaped capture on March 19-20: thirty-one

Captured and sent to Goliad, later executed on March 27: thirteen

Escaped and made their way to Victoria night of March 18: two

By March 16 Ward made it back to Goliad to report the failures of King and himself to an indecisive Fannin, still delaying his retreat to join Houston.[4]

From the Mexican perspective, Pena critically described the efforts of General Urrea to find and kill or capture the insurgents. " . . . He ordered Captain Pretalia with a small party of soldiers and thirty fellow townsmen to advance and delay the enemy until he could arrive with a force selected to give battle. He chose 100 horsemen and 180 infantrymen, and, with the only field piece he had, started the march; he traveled all night and at dawn on the 14th he found himself facing the enemy, who had been forced to halt at the mission of Refugio . . . He ordered an assault on the enemy, two hundred in number, who occupied a defensible position. It could not be taken because of the poor infantry destined for the sacrifice, who had been exhausted by the forced marches. . . . The result of General Urrea's attempt was a significant loss to us and none to the enemy, except six wounded." Pena continued, "While he was bent on fighting the force that had entrenched itself in the mission church, another one appeared at his rear guard, compelling him to send part of his reserve to face this new enemy. The latter had deployed himself in a wood, where a creek made him less accessible, so the general had to give up another part of his force; he ordered Colonel Garay to dislodge the enemy with sixty infantrymen. The thickness of the brush and density of the woods allowed us no further advantage than killing eleven and capturing seven, because daylight soon faded and the enemy, favored by darkness, fled. Those who remained enclosed (in the mission) had no food or water, and the general promised that they would surrender the next day or come out in open field and fight. They managed to escape nevertheless. . . . Our losses for this day were eleven dead and thirty-seven wounded, among them, three officers. At dawn on the 15th, when we took possession of the abandoned point, we found our wounded, some families of the colonists, and four of the enemy who had chosen not to follow their companions, as well as some compatriots of ours who had been impressed into enemy ranks. The general ordered all the cavalry at his disposal to chase the fugitives, costing the enemy sixteen dead and thirty-one prisoners on this day and fourteen on the following."[5]

(Note: Pena's figure of two hundred insurgents in the mission appears high since the total King/Ward force, before dividing, consisted of 28 men with King and 120 men with Ward.)

Earlier Houston had ordered Fannin to evacuate Goliad and fall back to Victoria. But the anxious Fannin vacillated, just as he had done about reinforcing the Alamo. With the loss of King and Ward, Fannin's force was depleted some 150 men as well as much of his wagon and cart transport. He spent March 18 taking "necessary measures for retreat in accordance with the resolution of the officers in council."[6]

At the same time, Mexican scouts were circling the La Bahia fortress, luring out Captain Albert C. Horton's enthusiastic but ineffective cavalrymen.

Despite the collective planning that must have ensued on the 18th, Fannin's men were overloaded with everything from personal effects to nine cannon and five hundred spare muskets. Houston ordered Fannin to dump the cannon in the river to expedite his movement but Fannin failed to do so.

Instead of leaving Goliad during the hours of darkness to attain a modicum of surprise, Fannin paused to burn Goliad houses and non-portable goods and equipment. The fires and smoke announced Fannin's departure to General Urrea as clearly as if he had sent a messager.

Since Fannin was the only insurgent commander with formal military training, his ineptitude is noteworthy. One author explained

" . . . young James did not perform well (at West Point), finishing his first year in the bottom half of his class. Partway through his second year he was put back into the starting class because of his poor academic performance. . . . Finally, after more than two years of poor progress, he submitted his resignation on October 25, 1821. . . . While at West Point, he learned little or nothing of the craft of war. . . . Still, in future years these facts would not keep him from claiming that he had acquired great military acumen during his abbreviated stint at West Point."[7]

Fannin was as unpopular with his troops as he was adept at making poor command decisions. One of the Alabama Red Rovers, A.J. Ferguson, wrote "Our commander is Col. Fannin, and I am sorry to say, the majority of the soldiers do not like him, for what cause I do not know, without it is because they think he has not the interest of the country at heart, or that he wishes to become great without taking the proper steps to attain greatness."[8]

In Fannin's fleeing but still feisty column on March 19 were the following units and numbers of men, totaling 500.[9]

(Note: No wonder Houston was anxious that Fannin's large force join him to bolster his Texas "Army")

Fannin's command group	9
The Georgia Battalion commander	1
Captain Horton's Mounted Rangers	51
Captain Bullock's Company (Texas Volunteers)	36
Captain Ticknor's Company (Texas Volunteers)	34
Captain Wadsworth's Company (Texas Volunteers)	26
Captain Winn's Company (Texas Volunteers)	34
The Lafayette Battalion commander	1
Captain Burke's Company (Mobile Greys)	34
Captain Duval's Company (Kentucky Mustangs)	45
Captain Pettus' Company (San Antonio Greys)	43
Captain Shackelford's Company (Red Rovers)	53
Captain Westover's Company (Regular Army)	42
Captain Wyatt's Company (Louisville Volunteers)	27
Fraser's Militia Company	39
Unassigned replacements	25

Horton's Mounted Rangers were the advance party of Fannin's column but it had gone no farther than a few miles when their hungry oxen stopped to graze. Then a howitzer cannon mired in the river, causing further delays. Several wagons broke down and they and their contents abandoned. By midmorning morale ebbed when someone discovered that most food and water had been left behind at Goliad, probably burned prior to their departure.

After marching some nine miles from Goliad, Fannin ordered a rest stop in a remarkably indefensible position—the middle of an open prairie. Captain/Doctor Jack Shackleford of the Alabama Red Rovers unsuccessfully argued with Fannin about the location, pointing out that only a few miles away was forested Coleto Creek, a much better place to halt and defend if necessary.

Suddenly Urrea's cavalry was galloping across the prairie behind, then encircling Fannin's column. He hastily formed them into a small rectangular defensive position. Heavily outnumbered, the advance guard of Horton's Rangers was cut off from the main body by the swift Mexican cavalry. Despite his orders and protestations, Horton's men rode away from the scene. His only recourse was to follow.

In retrospect, Horton's inability to reinforce Fannin at Coleto Creek is analagous to Fannin's failure to reinforce Travis at the Alamo. Would either Coleto or the Alamo have had a different outcome had those reinforcements arrived?

In Horton's case, his Rangers disobeyed his urging to break through the Mexican cavalry to aid the encircled Fannin. A lieutenant assumed command and led the Rangers toward Victoia and out of immediate danger. Fannin's troops reluctantly obeyed his decisions and were trapped in an indefensible position.

Doctor Joseph E. West, one of Fannin's surgeons who survived Goliad, described the dismal scene. "Our situation was very unfortunate, being in the midst of that large prairie, in a place where the ground was much lower than that around us. We were also without water, which is the greatest of necessities, especially for the wounded. The enemy having closed around us, upon every side, made a general charge but were repulsed with great slaughter. They rallied and charged again and again; but at every succeeding charge with less vigor, until night came and put an end to the carnage. The enemy retired to the woods in the direction of our march. When they had taken their position for the night, Col. Fanning (sic) ordered his men to prepare for resuming their march and cutting their way through the enemy's lines. But it was soon discovered, that so many of our horses were killed or wounded, and our oxen strayed away, that it was impossible to transport our wounded, who were more than sixty in number. Our commander said he would not leave them, but was resolved to share with them a common fate."[10]

Dawn only delivered more bad news, for the beleaguered insurgents soon learned that during the night Urrea had brought up reinforcements and three fieldpieces. Urrea recorded that "one hundred infantry, two four-pounders, and a howitzer were added to my force."

Doctor James H. Barnard, another surgeon with Fannin. wryly noted that the Mexicans "commenced the business of the day by treating us to a few rounds of grape and canister. . . . The rebels knew that their position was untenable; they could save their lives only by surrendering. The men agreed that they would lay down their arms only if Urrea granted them honorable terms. If he refused, they would fight to the death. Colonel Fannin limped forward under a flag of truce."[11]

Another of Fannin's surgeons who survived Goliad because of their ministrations for wounded Mexican officers was Doctor Joseph E. Fields. Fields' recollections of the surrender agreement between Urrea and Fannin are recorded in Fields' book "Three Years in Texas."

He wrote that "the articles of capitulation were soon agreed upon by the two commanders and committed to writing with the necessary signatures and formalities. The articles were, that in consideration of our surrendering, our lives should be ensured, our personal property restored, and that we were to be treated, in all respects, as prisoners of war are treated among enlightened nations. We also received a verbal promise to be sent, in eight days, to the nearest port, to be transported to the United States."

After conferring briefly with General Urrea, Fannin surrendered his 365 men of whom 97 were wounded including the thrice-wounded Fannin. Texan casualties were 27 killed in action. Mexican losses were only eleven killed and forty-nine wounded, according to Pena.

Urrea remembers the meeting with Fannin with some precision and defensiveness, contrary to Doctor Fields' account. "Addressing myself to Fannin and his companions . . . I said conclusively 'If you gentlemen wish to surrender at discretion, the matter is ended, otherwise I shall return to my camp and renew the attack.' . . . Had I been in a position to do so, I would have at least granted them their life. . . . about 400 prisoners fell into the hands of our troops. There were ninety-seven wounded, Fannin and several other leaders among them."[12]

Fannin returned to his troops, telling them their lives would be spared. They laid down their arms and were marched under guard back to the presidio of Goliad (La Bahia) where they were imprisoned. The ragged survivors of Ward's Georgia Battalion who had been captured at Dimitt's Landing soon joined the others at La Bahia.

Lending credence to Doctor Field's version of the surrender conditions Fannin, accompanied by Mexican Lieutenant Colonel Juan Jose Holzinger and a small party, left Goliad March 23 for the port at Copano to arrange for a ship to transport the prisoners back to the United States. Fannin returned to Goliad, having missed the expected ship at Copano. Apparently several of Urrea's officers also believed that the negotiated surrender terms accorded Fannin and his men prisoner of war status.

Regarding his dilemma with Fannin's surrender and Santa Anna's orders to kill all captured foreigners, Urrea wrote with an eye to the future. "(They) doubtlessly surrendered confident that Mexican generosity would not make their surrender useless, for under any other circumstances they would have sold their lives dearly, fighting to the last. I had due regard for the motives that induced them to surrender and for this reason I used my influence with the general-in-chief to save them, if possible, from being butchered, particularly Fannin. I obtained from His Excellency only a severe reply, repeating his previous order, *doubtless dictated by cruel necessity.*" (italics added)[13]

Many of the San Patricio, Refugio and Goliad survivors owed their lives to a brave, outspoken and beautiful lady, Francisca Alavez or Alvarez. She was the common-law wife of one of Urrea's cavalry officers, paymaster Captain Telesforo Alavez. At San Patricio she and Father Thomas Molloy interceded with General Urrea not to execute the prisoners taken there. One of Grant's command, Reuben R. Brown, recalled "I was taken out to be shot, but was spared through the interposition of a priest and a Mexican lady named Alvarez."

Eighty volunteers from Tennessee were captured by Mexican cavalry as they bathed in the Gulf of Mexico near Copano where they had just landed. Senora Alavez insisted the shrinking rawhide thongs around the prisoners' arms be loosened since they were painfully preventing circulation. Water was also provided the prisoners. Senora Alavez also acted as their intermediary before Lieutenant Colonel Nicholas de Portilla, successfully arguing that since the volunteers were unarmed they should not be executed.

At Goliad she intervened with Colonel Francisco Garay to spare as many of the prisoners as possible. Doctor James H. Barnard was one beneficiary, recording "a few of us, in consequence, were left to tell of that bloody day."

No wonder Francisca Alavez is dubbed "The Angel of Goliad" and a statue honoring her is outside La Bahia's walls. One story is that the captain, upon his return to Mexico City, abandoned "Panchita" Alavez. A happier version is that the couple lived in Matamoros after the war and had two children. The son, Matias, later worked for the King ranch in South Texas. Senora Alavez died on the ranch and was reportedly buried there, inexplicably, in an unmarked grave.

Urrea left Goliad in pursuit of other insurgents said to be in Victoria, probably Captain Horton's Mounted Rangers who had earlier led Fannin's disastrous march then escaped being encircled with the rest of Fannin's command. Perhaps Urrea's haste was to distance himself from Fannin and the prisoners at Goliad, knowing their eventual fate.

Left in charge of the prisoners at Goliad was Lieutenant Colonel Manuel Portilla, whose diary is quoted. "At daybreak (March 27, 1836, Palm Sunday) I decided to carry out the orders of the general-in-chief because I considered them superior. I assembled the whole garrison and ordered the prisoners, who were still sleeping, to be awaked. There were 445. The prisoners were divided into three groups and each was placed in charge of an adequate guard, the first under First Adjutant Agustin Alcerrica, the second under Capt. Luis Balderas, and the third under Captain Antonio Ramirez. I gave instructions to these officers to carry out the orders of the supreme government and the general-in-chief. This was immediately done. There was a great contrast in the feelings of the officers and men. Silence prevailed."[14]

Among the Tejanos was Francisco Garcia of Captain Horton's Mounted Rangers, who was spared execution March 27. Executed on that terrible day was Mariano Carbajal of Captain Pettus' Company. Paulino de la Garza and Jose Maria de la Garza, both of Fraser's Militia Company, were also executed.

Fannin was among the last of his men to be shot that morning. With musketry rattling in the background, a captain and six soldiers marched

Fannin to the northwest portion of the presidio yard. After hearing his one-sentence death sentence, Fannin produced his gold watch and asked the captain to present it to Portilla. The captain refused Fannin's request so he handed the watch to the captain with the understanding that his corpse would be buried and that he not be shot in the face. The captain agreed, also taking the monies Fannin emptied from his pockets.

Then Fannin was blindfolded and seated in a chair. The soldiers detached their bayonets from their muskets, then fired, on the captain's signal, at Fannin's head from a distance of about two feet.

The best estimate of the number of volunteers slaughtered that day is 342. Twenty-eight prisoners fortunately escaped death that terrible Palm Sunday.

Santa Anna's paltry defense of the Goliad massacre was "If, in the execution of law, no discretion is allowed a judge, can a general in a campaign be expected to execute greater freedom? The prisoners at Goliad were condemned by law, by a universal law, that of personal defense, enjoyed by all nations and individuals."[15]

Bodies were stripped and piled together. Some attempts were made to burn the bodies. Two months after the massacre their bodies were collected and buried by General Thomas Jefferson Rusk and his men on June 3, 1836. Secretary of War Rusk delivered the eulogy, which included the following.

"Fellow soldiers: In the order of Providence we are this day called upon to pay the last sad offices of respect to the remains of the noble and heroic band who, battling for our sacred rights, have fallen beneath the ruthless hand of a tyrant. Relinquishing the ease, the peace and the comforts of their homes, leaving behind them all they held dear—their mothers, sisters, daughters and wives—they subjected themselves to fatigue and privation, and nobly threw themselves between the people of Texas and the legions of Santa Anna."[16]

Fannin's repetitively poor decisions led to defeat and surrender of his men. Urrea was guilty of not pursuing with the general-in-chief his request for clemency for the prisoners and—knowing the outcome—leaving the scene prior to their slaughter. Santa Anna's barbarous cruelty on behalf of the Mexican army and Mexican people marked him, and them, forever. Santa Anna had provided two more Texan battle cries in addition to "Remember the Alamo!"

"Remember Goliad!" "Remember La Bahia!"

BATTLE OF COLETO: 2:30 p.m. MARCH 19, 1836

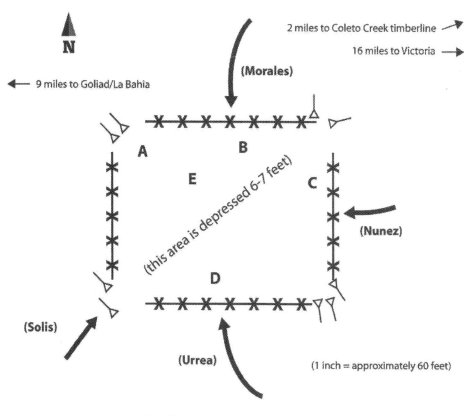

2 miles to Coleto Creek timberline

16 miles to Victoria

N

(Morales)

9 miles to Goliad/La Bahia

A

B

E

C

(this area is depressed 6-7 feet)

(Nunez)

D

(Solis)

(Urrea)

(1 inch = approximately 60 feet)

◁— Texas cannon

X X X Hasty barricade of wagons and dead livestock

◀— Mexican assault force

TEXAS FORCES
A - Red Rovers and San Antonio Greys
B - Mobile Greys
C - Kentucky Mustangs
D - Westover's Regulars
E - Fannin's position

THE ANGEL OF GOLIAD

This statue outside the walls of the Goliad Presidio
honors the memory of Senora Francisca Alavez. This heroic
and compassionate lady saved countless prisoners from
execution by the Mexican army. In the background is the
monument recognizing the Texas prisoners massacred at
Goliad on Palm Sunday, 1836.
(photo courtesy of N.K. Rogers)

CHAPTER TEN
HOUSTON'S RETREAT

After the tragic news of the Alamo's fall, Captain Juan Seguin began collecting recruits for his Tejano company at his ranch. With them, he arrived at Gonzales on March 6, following Fannin's earlier advice that he should report to General Houston. By March 12, Seguin's unit strength had increased to some 48 men.

Houston, still anxiously seeking the truth about the Alamo, sent famous scout Erastus "Deaf" Smith back to Bexar. Smith quickly returned on March 13 with Mrs. Susannah Dickinson (also spelled Dickenson) who told a tearful Houston about the slaughter of the Alamo defenders including her husband, Captain Almeron Dickinson.

Mrs. Dickinson warned Houston that Mexican troops were already at Cibolo Creek. Alarmed, he ordered an immediate retreat amid the hurried collection of rations and ammunition on oxen carts. Houston even ordered dumping two brass 24-pound cannon into the river rather than their possible breakdown hampering his hasty retreat.

Inhabitants of Gonzales, most of them already headed east on hearing the devastating rumors of the Alamo's fall and Santa Anna's advance, were further dismayed to look behind them and see their town in flames. Houston was leaving as little as possible that might benefit the Mexicans.

Families hurriedly gathered together what food and possessions they could carry or load onto wagons and began a fearful exodus to Louisiana or anywhere that seemed safe from Santa Anna's legions. Their frantic flight was unhappily called the "Runaway Scrape."

Houston had many detractors during his life but perhaps none so numerous nor caustic as during his retreat from Gonzales. One infantryman, Creed Taylor, who had earlier served with Jim Bowie, excoriated his general as follows. "Sam Houston had at Gonzales 500 men, of these at least one half of them had been at Concepcion and San Antonio, and he didn't have a man in his army who didn't have a blood grievance against the Mexicans and did not *know* that he could do as we have done before—whip ten-to-one of those carrion-eating convicts under Santa Anna.

"Let other historians rail and prate as they may but be it known to all future generations of Texas forth that if Jack Hays, John H. Moore or Old 'Paint' Caldwell had been in command at Gonzales on that fatal evening when Mrs. Dickinson brought the message of the Alamo's fall, the historians would have never heard of San Jacinto. Fanin (sic) and his men would have been saved—the butchery of Goliad averted and the 'Napoleon of the West' would have found his Waterloo. . . . The comrades assembled at Gonzales were there to *Fight* not to run."[1]

Seguin's men performed as the rear guard of Houston's army of some 374 mostly untrained, ill-equipped and poorly provisioned troops. Seguin's first sergeant was Manuel Flores, his brother-in-law. Another brother-in-law, Captain Salvador Flores, with twenty-five men of the Seguin company rode to ranches in the San Antonio River valley to evacuate and protect families there.

Amid the turmoil of evacuating, burning and providing a rear guard for Houston, Seguin still was able to send a message to Washington-on-the-Brazos to inform the Bexareno delegates, Ruiz and Navarro, of the fall of the Alamo

In San Antonio on March 14 Santa Anna ordered General of Brigade Antonio Ganoa's First Brigade to scour the area between San Antonio and the Colorado River for insurgents. General Urrea, Santa Anna's most capable general officer, was reinforced with several battalions of infantry and told to continue his thrust up the coast toward Galveston.

Later Santa Anna explained his rationale. " . . . The necessity of always choosing dispatch rather than any temporary advantage . . . determined me to divide my forces, after the capture of the Alamo, since our numbers permitted it, but in such a way that each division in itself should be able to cope with the enemy, whom I believed and now know positively, could not be numerous."[2]

On March 17 Houston reached Burnham's Ferry on the Colorado River with approximately 374 men. There the size of his force almost doubled by the infusion of volunteers. Houston happily anticipated the arrival of Fannin and four hundred more.[3]

Houston learned of the tragic news of the massacre of Fannin's command on March 23. He chose not to share the news of this massacre with his own reeling but growing force.

Had he intended to attack the Mexicans under General of Brigade Joaquin Ramirez y Sesma from the east bank of the swollen Colorado River at Burnham's Ferry, Houston changed his mind after hearing the debilitating news about Fannin. Burning the ferry, he marched his troops—many of who were adamant about attacking the Mexicans—down the east bank of the Colorado River to Beason's Crossing.

Among those angered at Houston's inaction on the Colorado was Sergeant Antonio Menchaca of Captain Seguin's Tejano company. "As soon as the Americans saw that the Mexicans were trying to draw them into an attack, the Americans prepared themselves to attack. But Houston told them that not a single man should move out, that the Mexicans were only trying to draw him out and ascertain his strength, which he did not intend to let them know."[4]

Again Houston's officers and troops urged attack. Prominent among them was just arrived Lieutenant Colonel Sydney Sherman of Kentucky. While sitting on the east bank of the Colorado, facing General Sesma on the opposite side, Houston implemented fundament drills and formations among his unhappy troops. Their anger became all the louder when he formed them into a column to once again retreat, this time towards San Felipe on the Brazos River.

Looking out for his own troops, Captain Seguin purchased twenty-two pair of shoes from merchant Joseph Urban of San Felipe. The shoes cost $2.00 each and Seguin paid the merchant with a promissory note.

Over two hundred angry and discouraged troops left Houston, either through furlough to assist their families or by desertion. One critic, Captain Robert Coleman, a veteran who had served at Concepcion and Bexar, chastised Houston as follows. "Thirteen hundred Americans retreating before a division of 800 Mexicans! Can Houston's strong partizans presume to excuse such dastardly cowardice under the pretence of laudable prudence?"[5]

Houston's troops entered San Felipe on March 28 but spent only one night there before veering twenty miles north to Jared Groce's plantation. Two company commanders flatly refused the order, preferring to defend the Brazos crossings at San Felipe and Fort Bend. Houston conceded to the two captains and his diminished army of about 500 men began the trek toward Groce's place.

Realizing he must address the mounting frustrations of his troops, Houston made a short speech. "My friends, I am told that evilly disposed persons have told you I am going to march you to the Redlands (the Nacogdoches area). This is false. I'm going to lead you into the Brazos bottom near Groce's to a position where you can whip the enemy even if he comes ten to one, and where we can get an abundant supply of corn."[6]

Captain Juan Seguin's company, now designated Company 9 (or "I" Company) of Sherman's Second Volunteer Texas Regiment, busily scouted and reported the activities of the Mexicans so well that Houston was never immediately threatened by his pursuers. Seguin's riders were not only superb horsemen but knew the surrounding country as well as they knew their own ranchos.

Seguin's company now numbered only twenty due to the splitting of the company with Captain Salvador Flores who was still operating among San Antonio's southern ranches. The official roster of Seguin's company, with original sequencing and spelling, is at Appendix D.

Houston's force had increased to about 1200 men by the time it reached the Colorado River on March 26 although many men were still deserting to locate and assist their families during the flood of refugees heading east.

On March 29 Santa Anna moved his main force out of Bexar toward Gonzales to locate and finally shatter Houston's retreating army.

On March 30 Houston's army had reached the Brazos River, near Groce's Crossing. A headcount revealed his strength had dropped to about 800. He made camp there, again began drill and rudimentary training for his soldiers, many of whom were still seething that Houston had refused to attack the Mexicans on the opposite side of the Colorado River.

Twelve days were spent at Groce's Crossing during which the Second Volunteer Texas Regiment was organized and Sidney Sherman promoted to colonel.

Hearing from his scouts and informers that Houston was now at Groce's plantation, Santa Anna left General Sesma at San Felipe. Santa Anna's destination was Harrisburg where scouts told him the Texas government had moved from Washington-on-the-Brazos. Considering the capture of Texas President David G. Burnet—and especially Texas Vice President Lorenzo de Zavala—more vital than smashing the apparently impotent Houston, Santa Anna struck out for Harrisburg. If he could capture Burnet, Zavala and cabinet, effectively the war would be over and he could return to Mexico City to the acclaim of the Mexican people.

Houston used his down time at Groce's to good purpose, training, drilling and resting his troops. Many of his soldiers were ill or injured and received medical attention at the plantation home of wealthy Jared Groce. The almost two weeks at Groce's plantation improved the morale of Houston's troops but not their distrust of their general as a combat leader. Even the interim Texas government was nursing third and fourth thoughts about Houston's resolve. General Rusk, the Secretary of War, was sent to Groce's for a showdown with Houston. The government letter he bore was to the point about Houston's deficiencies. "Sir: The enemy are laughing you to scorn. You must fight them. You must retreat no further. The country expects you to fight. The salvation of the country depends on your doing so."[7]

On April 12, Houston and his army broke camp at Groce's and resumed their march to the southeast. A few days later, the Texas column approached a now famous fork in the road in what is now Harris County. Toward the left was east Texas, Nacogdoches (also called the Redlands) and safety. Instead, if Houston ordered the column to the right, his army would be heading toward Harrisburg and a showdown with Santa Anna.

Several of his commanders previously warned Houston that he must take the right fork or they would take over the army themselves. The troops, well aware of Houston's tendency to show the enemy his back, began chanting "go right, go right." A local resident, Abram Roberts, stood by his gate, pointing to the Harrisburg turn. Houston's miniscule band of four pipers and two drummers began playing and took the turn to the right. The cheering soldiers followed.

Riding in the middle of the column, Houston gave no commands and displayed no reaction as the column turned right, forcing their general and themselves to eventual battle with the Mexicans instead of safety in Louisiana.

An angry confrontation with Mrs. Pamelia Mann indicated Houston had planned to take the left turn to Nacogdoches rather than the turn to Harrisburg. Mrs. Mann had loaned Houston a pair of oxen to help pull his two six-pound cannon, the prized and newly arrived "Twin Sisters." Earlier, she told Houston that he could use the oxen "if you are going on to the Nacogdoches Road."

When the army took the right turn toward Harrisburg, Mrs. Mann caught up with Houston. "General, you told me a damn lie! You said that (you) was going on the Nacogdoches Road. Sir, I want my oxen." With that she cut the oxens' leads with a butcher knife and rode off, leading them.

On April 14 Santa Anna's capture of the Texas cabinet failed and, chagrinned, he burned Harrisburg on April 18 and moved on to New Washington. There he again failed to capture President Burnet and his cabinet who narrowly escaped Colonel Juan N. Almonte's cavalry. Seeing women with the cabinet in the fleeing schooner *Flash*, gentlemanly Colonel Almonte gave the order to cease fire, so Burnet's group escaped to Galveston Island. After two days rest and rampage, Mexican troops fired New Washington as well as the Point Morgan plantation home and storehouses of Colonel James Morgan. Here, so the story goes, lovely Miss Emily D. West, "The Yellow Rose of Texas," was captured by the Mexicans. In Santa Anna's silken tent at San Jacinto she diverted her captor's attention during the Texas surprise assault at San Jacinto.

While Santa Anna planned the capture of the Texas cabinet, Houston received important intelligence April 18 when "Deaf" Smith and others captured a Mexican officer bearing official letters contained in saddlebags once belonging to Travis. The letters revealed that General Cos would soon reinforce Santa Anna's force of about 600 with 650 more. At that time, Houston's effective strength was over 1,000, so he had numerical superiority over Santa Anna if he could engage Santa Anna before Cos' announced arrival at Lynch's Ferry on Buffalo Bayou.

Once in Harrisburg, Houston revealed his bias when he "ordered Sherman to have the Mexican (Seguin's Tejanos) company left at camp, that they knew little about fighting, but were good at herding. General Sherman went to the 'Mexican company' and asked for Captain Seguin and was told he was not there. Then General Sherman instructed me (Sergeant Antonio Menchaca) that as soon as Captain Seguin came, to tell them that his company was ordered to remain and guard horses and equipages."[8]

Angered by the Sherman/Houston order, Menchaca convinced Seguin that they should personally appeal the order to Houston. Later standing before Houston, Menchaca vented his anger. "I did not enlist to guard horses and would not do such duty." Menchaca wanted to fight, even if he died "facing the enemy." Impressed by such candor and dedication, Houston relented. "I do not see why you should not be allowed to fight." He also suggested that the Tejanos place a piece of cardboard in their hats to distinguish themselves from Mexican soldiers.

While crossing Buffalo Bayou below Harrisburg, Captain Seguin noticed a young boy, who turned out to be a sixteen-year old orphan, joining the Texans as a cart driver. Seguin described the boy as dressed in Mexican clothing but looking more like an Indian. The lad's name was Juan Lopez and he joined Seguin's men as they rafted the bayou. Juan Lopez became the youngest and latest recruit of the Seguin company, now twenty-one strong, as it approached the San Jacinto plain.

Sergeant Menchaca recalled that crossing the swollen bayou by raft was not completed until about 5:00 on the evening of April 19.

Captain Seguin remembered "At daybreak a man was taken prisoner, who, on discovering us, attempted to escape. He was a printer belonging to San Felipe, and informed us that the enemy were at a distance of about 8 miles, on the way back to Harrisburg. Our scouts came in soon with the information that the enemy were countermarching towards Buffalo Bayou."[9]

Houston's army, some 783 men, spread itself on the northern end of the San Jacinto plain among a stand of live oaks bordering Buffalo Bayou. As a defensive position, his choice was not much better than Fannin's at Coleto Creek. Houston's position was bounded by water on two sides. The enemy's probable position to his front would prevent Houston's being reinforced, supplied or evacuated. As for retreat

Houston ordered Erastus "Deaf" Smith to destroy Vince's Bridge to the southwest. Lynch's Ferry in the opposite direction was both too far and too small to accommodate a quick escape. Rafting Buffalo Bayou again with an enemy shooting at their heels might be disastrous for Houston's men.

Captain Seguin described his company's first encounter with the enemy on the plain. "We were beginning to cook our meal, when the enemy showed themselves close to us. We rushed to arms, and formed in line of battle. On their nearer approach we were ordered to lay down on the ground, thus concealing ourselves in the grass. A height, adjacent to our position, was soon occupied by the enemy, upon which the General ordered the band to strike up 'Will you come to the bower.' The enemy answered with its artillery, and we joined the chorus with a brisk musketry. We were soon charged by a skirmishing party on foot, detached from the right wing of the enemy; they were quickly driven back by a party of our cavalry, supported by the artillery. The enemy kept up their fire until they selected a camping ground, about four hundred steps away from ours and protected by two motts (small stands of trees). Both armies ceased firing; we resumed the cooking of our meal . . ."[10]

Santa Anna had begun marching northward toward San Jacinto on the morning of April 20, the burning settlement of New Washington where he had spent two days at his back.

After an initial exchange of cannon fire and cavalry skirmishing, Mexican infantry edged forward toward the Texas positions. Sergeant Menchaca of Seguin's company remembered Houston's peculiar "orders that those men who lived upon the Navidad and Lavaca (rivers) and killed deer at a hundred paces offhand should come forward and take a shot at the Mexicans." One round was allowed each of the fifty sharpshooters who came forward, formed a line and fired their single round of ammunition.

Having acknowledged the other's presence, the two armies settled down behind their positions separated by a mile of open prairie on the small plain of San Jacinto.

Santa Anna's camp was established on a small knoll. Ahead of his position was the open prairie to the left. To his right was a wooded area behind which began a marsh extending to the rear, as well as a small lake named Peggy. Mexican soldiers worked well into the night building a hasty breastwork of saddles and supply wagons. Santa Anna's own silken tent was erected under a few hardwood trees.

The circular shaped breastworks dominating the Mexican sector extended northeast from the New Washington road on the left to the swamps on the right. The entire defensive line was approximately one and one-half miles in length. Placed along this line (from left to right) were Santa Anna's cavalry, infantry (the Matamoros Battalion), the single nine-pound brass cannon dubbed the "Golden Standard" and the remainder of the Matamoros Battalion on the right flank. Behind his right flank infantry, Santa Anna positioned five companies. Another five companies of grenadiers were behind the left flank. Santa Anna's reserve, if it can be called that, initially consisted only of himself and his staff, in the rear.

Mexican Sergeant Becerra, recollecting San Jacinto, added a social note as well as a prophecy. "A few days before the battle of San Jacinto General Santa Anna and General Castrillon, second in command, had a misunderstanding, and General Castrillon formed a mess of his own, and he took his cook with him, which was a great inconvenience to Santa Anna, as he had no cook of his own. This quarrel was not settled. They went into battle with angry feelings. . . . General Castrillon criticized General Santa Anna's disposition of the Mexican troops at San Jacinto, and predicted a defeat."[11]

CHAPTER ELEVEN
"WILL YOU COME TO THE BOWER I HAVE SHADED FOR YOU?"

Around 9:00 on the morning of April 21, General Cos' reinforcing column of four battalions arrived amid the blare of bugles, increasing Santa Anna's strength to 1200-1300 men. After welcoming his brother-in-law, Santa Anna pointed to an area behind his defensive line in the right rear where Cos' exhausted men could rest.

Apparently Houston chose to delay his attack until after Cos had arrived, thinking that Cos' arrival during a battle might undermine the morale of his feisty Texans. He held a meeting with his senior officers around noon to discuss the timing of their attack. Most of his officers seemed to agree on an attack the next day.

Houston made no decision until his troops, hearing of the meeting, threatened to mutiny unless Houston attacked immediately. "Very well," he calmed them. "Get your dinners and I will lead you into the fight and if you whip the enemy every one of us shall be a captain."[1]

After visiting his twenty troops busily checking their weapons and placing pieces of cardboard on their hats and chests to distinguish them from the Mexicans, Seguin went to his tent. While having his own "dinner" he was joined by General Thomas Rusk, the Secretary of War. After finishing their meal Rusk inquired if Mexican troops normally took a siesta after lunch. Seguin answered yes but armed sentinels were posted during these times.

Seguin's memory of the assault lends a perspective more direct than most. "General Rusk observed that he thought so, too, however the moment seemed to him favorable to attack the enemy. He added: 'Do you feel like fighting?' I answered that I was always ready and willing to fight, upon which the general rose, saying 'Well, let us go!' I made my dispositions at once."[2]

Soon after his decision to attack, coerced by the threat of mutiny from his troops, Houston asked Lieutenant Colonel Joseph Bennett to visit the companies and see if the men were ready. "I reported back to him and said the men were ready to fight," Bennett recalled. "Houston then ordered the troops to be paraded (formed)."[3]

Houston's thin, two-row battle line consisted of Sherman's Second Regiment (containing Seguin's Tejano company) on his left. Next was Burleson's First Regiment, then the "Twin Sisters" six-pound cannon given Texas by the citizens of Cincinnati, Ohio. Millard's Texas Regular Battalion was on the right and on the far right flank was Lamar's cavalry.

Houston guided his horse to the center of the line, a bit forward of the first rank. At 3:30, he unsheathed his sword, commanded "Trail arms! Forward!" and led his army into the fray. Once the firing started, two drummers and four fifers began playing the same tune they had performed at the famous fork in the road leading them to San Jacinto. A member of the "band" was Tejano Martin Flores, a fifer of Captain Briscoe's company. The tune they played was a lilting, bawdy song popular among the troops.

"Will you come to the bower I have shaded for you?

Our bed shall be roses all spangled with dew,

There under the bow'r on roses you'll lie,

With a blush on your cheek but a smile in your eye!"

Oddly, the Mexican sentries' customary cries of "centinela alerta!" were quiet. Why those sentinels manning Santa Anna's defensive line didn't immediately see Houston's ragged army advancing across the prairie is unknown. Most of the Mexican troops probably were sleeping or resting near their weapons.

So were their officers, Santa Anna among them enjoying his tent and, perhaps, the company of young, beautiful Emily Morgan, the "Yellow Rose of Texas."

By 4:30 the Texas assault line was still undetected some 550 yards from the Mexican positions. The silent advancing line of Texans hesitated as a bugle sounded from the right flank of the Matamoros Battalion, stretched out along the entire defensive line. Other buglers took up the alarm and the Mexican cannon crew manning the Golden Standard fired a hasty round of grapeshot. The grapeshot and the few rifle rounds fired by startled soldiers of the Matamoros Battalion mostly went over the heads of the advancing Texans.

The first Mexican general officer aware of the threat was General Fernandez Castrillon who was shaving. Grabbing his sword, he attempted to rally the line and bring up reinforcements from the Aldama Battalion.

Texas artillery, the six-pound Twin Sisters, had been manhandled out in front of the line of advancing infantrymen and began firing from about 200 yards at the Mexican position. Overtaken by their infantrymen, the Twin Sisters again were pushed forward to within 70 yards of the Mexicans and commenced firing again. Santa Anna's only cannon, the nine-pound Golden Standard, fired three hasty rounds without effect and was loaded for a fourth round before being overrun by the rampaging Texans of the First and Second Regiments.

The Texas Regular Battalion surged forward, so did Lamar's cavalry which overran the grenadiers Santa Anna had positioned behind and on his left flank.

Seguin recounted his part in the assault. "We marched out onto the prairie and were met by a column of infantry, which we drove back briskly. Before engaging that column, we had dispersed an ambuscade that had opened fire against us within pistol shot. The entire enemy line, panic struck, took to flight."[4]

Corporal Ambrosio Rodriguez remembered First Sergeant Manuel Flores yelling at his men "Get up, you cowards! Santa Anna's men are running!"

Seguin noticed Juan Lopez, who had informally joined his Tejanos at the Buffalo Bayou crossing, waving an old sword and a stick with a red rag tied to its end. Seguin ordered Lopez to take the musket from

Private Manuel Tarin, who was too ill to fight. Juan Lopez, armed with Tarin's musket, distinguished himself throughout the engagement.

Shortly thereafter a Mexican officer pleaded with Sergeant Antonio Menchaca that he was a brother Mexican and to spare his life. "I'm an American!" Menchaca replied. Then to another soldier Menchaca yelled "Shoot him!" The soldier did, killing the officer. In later years, Menchaca appeared not to remember this poignant incident. He did recall requiring his men to place large pieces of white cardboard on their hats and chests.

Many of the Mexican soldiers jumped into Peggy's Lake for safety but were shot down. Seguin ordered his men to cease fire when another officer, hidden in bushes beside the lake, called out and asked to be spared. That officer surrendered to Seguin and was closely followed by several others. Among Seguin's officer prisoners were Colonel Juan Almonte, Colonel Juan Maria Bringas, a Colonel Dias and several others.

General Castrillon tried to rally his demoralized men, even climbing atop an ammunition box. General Rusk attempted to save the wounded general but his troops ignored him, shooting and yelling "Remember the Alamo!" "Remember Goliad!" "Remember La Bahia!"

Colonel Pedro Delgado remembered in terrible detail the rout of his soldados from the hasty barricade they had prepared the previous night from wagons, boxes and pack saddles. " . . . I saw our men flying in small groups, terrified, and sheltering themselves behind large trees. I endeavored to force some of them to fight, but all efforts were in vain, the evil was beyond remedy. They were a bewildered, panic-stricken herd.

The enemy kept up a brisk crossfire of grape on the woods. Presently we heard in close proximity the unpleasant noise of their clamors.

Meeting no resistance, they dashed lightening-like upon our deserted camp.

Then I saw his excellency (Santa Anna) running about in utmost excitement. Wringing his hands and unable to give an order. . . . Everything was lost. I went, leading my horse—which I could not mount, as the firing had rendered him restless and fractious—-to join our men, still hoping that we might be able to defend ourselves or to retire under shelter of the night. This, however, could not be done. It is a known fact that Mexican soldiers, once demoralized, cannot be controlled unless they are thoroughly inured to war. On the left, and about a musket-shot distant from our camp, was a small grove on the bay shore. Our disbanded herd rushed to it to obtain shelter from the horrid slaughter carried out on all over the prairie by the bloodthirsty usurpers. Unfortunately we met in our way an obstacle hard to overcome. It was a bayou, not very wide, but rather deep. The men, on reaching it, would hopelessly crowd together, and were shot down by the enemy, who was close enough to not miss his aim. It was there the greatest carnage took place."[5]

Mexican soldiers fleeing to the rear disrupted the three battalions trying to close ranks and fight. Soon most Mexicans were surging to the rear. Running from his tent, Santa Anna reportedly grabbed another man's horse and rode away wearing bedroom slippers and a silken shirt with diamond cuff links. He was immediately followed by his personal secretary, Martinez Caro.

There was no stopping the slaughter although many officers, including Houston, tried. The battle itself was over in eighteen minutes but the carnage continued for another hour.

Mexican losses were 600-650 killed and 730 taken prisoner. An estimated 70 or 80 Mexicans escaped the slaughter. Texas losses were small: eight men killed or soon died of wounds and 18 wounded.[6]

Another historian reported Texan losses as nine killed in action and 34 wounded.[7]

Houston was wounded in the left leg and ankle. In Seguin's company, only newly joined Private Juan Lopez was slightly wounded in his left knee.

The next morning a small, disheveled Mexican dressed in the blue tunic of a private was captured near Vince's Bridge which "Deaf" Smith and his six men earlier had destroyed. The prisoner claimed to be a private.

Back at the prisoner enclosure several captured Mexicans called the new arrival "El Presidente." His own troops spoiled Santa Anna's disguise. Wisely, Houston prevented his Texans from lynching Santa Anna on the spot.

Sergeant Menchaca served as interpreter for Houston's questioning of Santa Anna. Menchaca also procured a hot meal for the famished prisoner and talked to Santa Anna at length about the latter's experiences during the Mexican revolution.

Santa Anna later penned his alibis for the defeat. " . . . It never crossed my mind that a moment of rest, now indispensable, should have been so disastrous, particularly after I had issued orders of strict vigilance to insure our safety. . . . My sleep was interrupted by the noise of arms, and upon awakening, I saw with astonishment that the enemy had completely surprised our camp."[8]

By specious reasoning, Santa Anna blamed newly arrived General Cos for the debacle. "If then, everything was favorable, if everything had been foreseen, and the operation well-conducted, what was the cause of the fateful defeat of San Jacinto? It was the excessive number of raw recruits in the five hundred men under the command of General Cos."[9]

Lieutenant Colonel Pena repeats a witness' concise description of Santa Anna's defeat " . . . that the defeat was by surprise and that the greater part of our forces perished. He left the battlefield the following day, and he assures me that it had not lasted even half an hour, that the troops hardly had time to fall in ranks, and that a very few of the select companies were the only ones to give battle. He states that the division of the president-general, in the position it occupied had a wooded area to its right and a lake at its rear, leaving the left as its only avenue of retreat; that the enemy advanced frontally with a body of infantry, two artillery pieces, and its cavalry to the left, in order to attract attention while the main body of the troops marched hidden behind tall grass in order to flank our right, which they managed to do; that our troops were surrounded in a few moments, and since all was confusion and disorder, most of them were pushed into the lagoon; and that those who could escape fled toward the position we occupied on the Brazos, but, finding the bridge burned at Buffalo Bayou and unable to cross it, our soldiers were overtaken by the enemy, who wreaked on them a horrible carnage to avenge themselves for those we had executed."[10]

Other than the members of Captain Seguin's Company "I" at least five other Tejanos fought at the battle of San Jacinto. They were Major Lorenzo de Zavala, Jr., Houston's aide-de-camp; Peter Lopez of Captain Karnes cavalry troop; Martin Flores, fifer, of Captain Briscoe's Regulars; Antonio Trevino of Captain Baker's San Felipe Company; and Jose Molino from Nacogdoches. The latter's real name was Jose Palonio Lavigna.

Later General Houston wrote a short accolade on the performance of Captain Seguin and "I" Company. "The Colonel commanded the only Mexican company who fought in the cause of Texas at the Battle of San Jacinto. His chivalrous and estimable conduct in the battle won for him my warmest regard and esteem." Years later, Houston wrote Erasmo Seguin and spoke again about Juan's conduct and that of "his brave company in the army of 1836, and his brave and gallant bearing in the battle of San Jacinto, with that of his men."

The famous cannon at the battle of San Jacinto, the Twin Sisters of the Texans and the Golden Standard of the Mexicans, have been subject of many investigations. One story about the Twin Sisters is that they were dug up at La Bahia/Goliad in 1936 and now rest on the graves of the Goliad massacred volunteers alongside the San Antonio River.

The captured Golden Standard cannon may have been mounted on the Texas Navy warship *Independence*. On April 17, 1837, the *Independence* was chased, badly shot-up, eventually surrendering to the two Mexican warships disabling her near the Brazos River. The *Independence* was the only Texas Navy warship to have surrendered during the history of the Texas Navy.

It was a singular prize for the Mexicans. Onboard the battered ship was the Texas minister to the U.S. who had negotiated U.S. recognition of the new Republic of Texas. Despite his diplomatic status William H. Wharton was taken prisoner and imprisoned in Matamoros, Mexico. To the Mexicans' delight, they also discovered a "nine-pound long brass pivot gun" believed to be the Golden Standard, captured by Sam Houstons's small army at the battle of San Jacinto a year earlier.

With suitable pomp, the Golden Standard cannon was escorted by the Mexican warships back to their home port of Vera Cruz where it was joyfully and ceremoniously received.

Appendix G contains this and other versions of what may have happened to those famous cannon of the revolution.

BATTLE OF SAN JACINTO: 3:30 p.m. APRIL 21, 1836

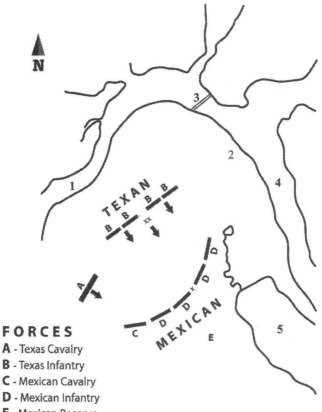

FORCES

A - Texas Cavalry
B - Texas Infantry
C - Mexican Cavalry
D - Mexican Infantry
E - Mexican Reserve
X - Cannon

OBSTACLES

1 - Buffalo Bayou
2 - Swamp
3 - Lynch's Ferry
4 - San Jacinto River
5 - Peggy's Lake

(1 inch = approx. 1/2 mile)

CHAPTER TWELVE
FRIEND, NOW FOE?

Under the terms of the Articles of Agreement signed at San Jacinto and the two Velasco Treaties between Texas and Mexico, Santa Anna ordered Generals Filisola, Urrea, Ramirez y Sesma and Gaona to evacuate Texas and return their commands to Monterrey.

Santa Anna and his generals also "solemnly acknowledge, sanction and ratify, the full, entire, and perfect independence of the Republic of Texas." (Article 4). In Article 10 they also pledged to not "take up arms against the people of Texas, or any portion of them, and will consider themselves bound, by every sacred obligation, to abstain from all hostility towards Texas or its citizens."

Once back in Mexico City, Santa Anna had no intention of keeping his pledge not to "Take up arms against the people of Texas." Three times Mexico invaded Texas, trying to reclaim it.

First was General Rafael Vasquez raiding San Antonio in March, 1842. He took a few prisoners and cattle and returned to Mexico unchallenged by the surprised Bexarenos.

The following June Colonel Antonio Canales led a cavalry troop across the Nueces River to steal livestock. This time the Texans were more alert and repulsed Canales at a skirmish at Fort Lipanitlan near Corpus Christi in South Texas.

A larger force of about 1400 men under General Adrian Woll crossed the Rio Grande River on August 31, awakened and occupied San Antonio on Sunday, September 11. By noon Woll's soldiers had captured some sixty-two Texans.

A call for assistance to citizens at Gonzales, Victoria, Black Jack Springs and Seguin met with success and a Texas camp was established at Salado Creek near New Braunfels.

In a daring move to draw out Woll and his men from San Antonio and into the Salado prairie, Texans rode into the town's main plaza shooting pistols and defying Woll's troops. By afternoon about 1200 Mexicans were engaging the Texans on the Salado.

In a separate action some fifty-three volunteers from Black Jack Springs on their way to the Salado were encircled by Mexican cavalry and nearly annihilated. Thirty-six were killed in action and another fifteen wounded were captured. Only two Texans escaped.

At the Salado battle site, the Texas forces prevailed. One Texan was killed as were an estimated sixty of Woll's soldados. Woll also suffered approximately 200 wounded. Claiming a victory, Woll led his remaining troops back to San Antonio, then began returning to Mexico by Monday, chased by Texans. Among the Texas victors was the indomitable Antonio Menchaca who had fought beside Captain Seguin at San Jacinto. Menchaca was wounded while battling Woll's troops in San Antonio. Another Tejano, intrepid Salvadore Flores, successfully led a group of 100 men against Woll's invading army.)

After San Jacinto Houston ordered Captain Seguin and company to follow the Mexican army to prevent its looting and stealing citizens' property on the way to the Rio Grande River. Seguin also had to contend with the wounded and sick left behind by the retreating Mexicans.

If that assignment was not daunting enough, Seguin was ordered to garrison San Antonio, accept the Mexican surrender of Bexar and raise a battalion of volunteers to defend "the frontier." He led his small band of twenty-two soldiers into San Antonio on June 4, 1836 and set to work restoring order.

Unable to enlist the requisite ninety men for a battalion, Seguin asked General Rusk, now the commander of the Texas army, for reinforcements. Rusk dispatched 180 men for temporary duty to bolster Seguin's force but short-term aid was inadequate to enable Seguin to amply defend San Antonio against further Mexican incursions.

On June 21 Seguin notified the Bexarenos that he must evacuate the town. He instructed them to accompany him to the interior, taking with them all livestock to keep it from the Mexicans.

The citizens of Bexar ignored Seguin's order and were awakened in October by a troop of Mexican cavalry searching for cattle. After a furlough from the army to care for his own family, Seguin was again ordered to garrison San Antonio. He was promoted to lieutenant colonel on September 17 and succeeded in raising a battalion of 80 men by November.

Despite lack of support or funding from the Texas army, Seguin accomplished his Bexar mission as long as possible. He lost favor among many Bexarenos since he was forced to confiscate city funds as well as horses and mules for the benefit of his soldiers whom he described to General Albert S. Johnston as "chiefly on foot, naked and barefoot".

In October, several changes in the Texas command structure would bedevil Seguin. Sam Houston had been elected President of Texas and General Rusk resumed his former job as Secretary of War. In Rusk's place as commander of the Texas army was Felix Huston, an American adventurer who arrived after San Jacinto. General Huston complained to Houston about Seguin's competence as a commander, criticizing "he cannot speak our language."

In early 1837, General Huston ordered Lieutenant Colonel Seguin to evacuate *and destroy* San Antonio. Seguin penned an appeal, gave it to cousin Blas Herrera to deliver to President Houston and awaited the reply.

Houston revoked Huston's order but Seguin had made an important and powerful enemy for life. He opined that Huston's purpose was to buy up San Antonio land cheaply once the city was abandoned. Seguin again withdrew from San Antonio and took a longer furlough, not returning to Bexar until March 1838.

Land speculation, fraudulent claims, even theft were rampant during this period. Many Tejanos had received land grants as a reward for their services to revolutionary Texas. Unscrupulous Americans, some just arrived, successfully offered poor families a pittance for their lands. False claims and false testimony concerning land rights and transfers were commonplace. Juan Seguin was not above dabbling in land. At one time he held ten certificates or land grants, usually in the amount of 640 acres each.

Land was not the only tempting target for the underhanded. So was livestock. "After the disbandment of the army, many of the cattle beyond the Nueces (River) were rounded up by discharged soldiers, adventurers and other enterprising Texans for private ownership to replace losses sustained during the revolution, or to drive to markets as far east as New Orleans and Natchez."

"The Texas 'cowboys' raiding into the area west of the Nueces, drove out cattle from the Mexican ranches at Viejo, Anaquitas, Las Animas, San Juan de Carricitos, Norias, San Antonio, Los Fresnos, Colorado, El Mulato, Jaboncillos, Santa Rosa, Mota, Santa Margarita, Santa Gertrudis, San Diego, Los Angeles, El Pato, La Pavida, San Patricio, Salmoneno and others, some of which had been abandoned. Occasionally the raiders were excused on the grounds that the Consultation at San Felipe in November, 1835, had decreed that all persons leaving the country without permission from the proper authorities, to avoid participation in the 'struggle' with Mexico, would forfeit all or any lands they may hold or may have claim to, for the benefit of the government."[1]

The later Texas Constitution contained a similar proviso.

Upon his return, Seguin was surprised to find he had been elected by the citizens of Bexar to be their senator to the Congress of Texas. Resigning his commission, he rode to Houston, the new capital, and there assumed his duties. As the first Tejano senator, he fought to represent not only his Bexar constituents but all Tejanos. As the Republic of Texas grew so did Seguin's fears that Tejanos were being overlooked and excluded from their new government.

Addressing the Texas Senate in February 1840, Seguin questioned the application of the appropriation of $15,000. for Spanish translation of laws so they could be understood by all. His words were a reminder that Tejanos were first class citizens whose contributions toward Texas independence were being forgotten by their new government.

"Mr. President, the dearest rights of my constituents as Mexico-Texians are guaranteed by the Constitution and the laws of the Republic of Texas; and at the formation of the social compact between the Mexicans and the Texians, they had rights guaranteed to them, they also contracted certain legal obligations—of all of which they are ignorant, and in consequence of their ignorance of the language in which the Laws and Constitution of the land are written. The Mexico-Texians were among the first who sacrificed their all in our glorious Revolution, and the disasters of war weighed heavily upon them, to achieve these blessings which, it appears, are destined to be the last to enjoy, and as a representative from Bexar, I never shall cease to raise my voice in effecting this object."[2]

Not only Seguin, but all Texans should have been enraged when Sam Houston, the hero of San Jacinto, former President of the Republic of Texas and now a United States Senator representing Texas, was quoted in the *New York Herald* of January 30, 1848. "Mexicans are no better than Indians. I see no reason why we should not . . . take their land."

Seguin's several commercial enterprises cost him more disfavor among Bexarenos and newcomers who now considerably outnumbered the original citizens of the town. Seguin's adventures with the "Republic of the Rio Grande" and the doomed Santa Fe Expedition added to his unpopularity.

In early 1842, Seguin was elected alcalde or mayor of Bexar. However, growing rumors over his supposed friendship with Mexican authorities, specifically General Rafael Vasquez, caused former hero, senator, and alcalde Seguin to retire to his ranch.

Now often unjustly labelled traitor, Seguin's life as well as those of his family were threatened. Disheartened by the rumors and ill treatment, Seguin decided to "seek a refuge among my enemies, braving all dangers."[3]

He resigned as alcalde, explaining "unable any longer to suffer the persecutions of some ungrateful Americans who strove to murder me, I had determined to free my family and friends from their continual misery on my account, and go and live peaceably in Mexico."[4]

On arriving with his family in Nuevo Laredo, Mexico, Seguin was imprisoned, then sent to Monterrey. Instead of being allowed to retire in Saltillo where he had family, Seguin was to be taken to Mexico City but, fortunately, the order was revoked. Seguin was given the choice to remain in prison, his family impoverished, or "return to Texas with a company of explorers to attack its citizens and, by spilling my blood, vindicate myself."[5]

The maliciousness shown Seguin—for whom the Texas town is named—by former comrades and friends was repeated time and again to other Tejano families.

The family of Martin de Leon, a colonizer or empresario like Austin, was the another collective victim of prejudice and malice. The de Leon family had been singled out by Mexican General Urrea during his campaign for its support of the revolution. After the revolution the de Leons were again assailed. But this time their detractors were former Texas friends and comrades whom the de Leons previously had assisted.

A Texan reportedly rustling livestock murdered Agapito de Leon. Silvestre de Leon, on the way to sell cattle, was ambushed and robbed. Fernando de Leon was wounded in a similar fracas. There were no criminal charges filed nor the guilty sought in these incidents, mute testimony to the prevailing lawlessness and animosity toward Tejanos.

The de Leons and Carvajals fled to Louisiana for safety and remained there for several years. Patricia de la Garza de Leon and family eventually returned to Texas to reclaim their properties but met with limited success.

Placido Benavides, who had organized Tejano companies alongside Juan Seguin, was another ostracized hero. Preferring that Texas become an independent state in the Mexican federation, Benavides retired to his ranch near Guadalupe Victoria. Try as he might, he was unable to distance himself from the revolution after he aided a Goliad survivor, Isaac Hamilton of the Alabama Red Rovers When Urrea's lancers came searching for the wounded Hamilton, found hidden in his wagon, Benavides had no option other than surrendering him. Hamilton was to become one of the beneficiaries of Francisca Alavez, "The Angel of Goliad." He was spared execution due to her intervention.

As soon as he landed in Mexico, Santa Anna repudiated his surrender and pledged to restore Texas to Mexico. Three times Santa Anna sent invading forces back into Texas. In the Articles of Agreement signed at San Jacinto, Santa Anna swore he would not "on any occasion whatever, take up arms against the people of Texas.or any portion of them, but will consider themselves (Santa Anna and his generals) by every sacred obligation, to abstain from all hostility towards Texas or its citizens."

In Mexico City Santa Anna was preoccupied by internal affairs, including later repulsing a French attack on Vera Cruz in 1838, and maintaining his own political power.

Almost insolvent but still independent, the Republic of Texas somehow prevailed. The patriotism, courage and steadfastness of Tejanos like Seguin, Benavides, and Zavala, among many others, contributed to that success.

The tribute paid to Zavala in the *Telegraph and Texas Register* upon his November 15, 1836 death are equally applicable to all those Tejanos and Tejanas participating in the revolution.

" . . . Texas has lost one of her most valuable citizens, the cause of liberal principles one of its most untiring advocates, and society one of its brightest ornaments."

God and Liberty! Dios y libertad!

To see how the Texas revolution is presented in one public school history text, see Appendix H.

APPENDIX A
THE CONSTITUTION OF THE MEXICAN UNITED STATES (with original spelling)

Given in Mexico, 4th October, 1824, fourth year of Independence, third of Liberty, and second of the Federation. Signed by the Members of Congress and the Supreme Executive Power.

The Supreme Executive Power, provisionally appointed by the general sovereign Congress of the Nation, to all who shall see these presents, know, and understand, that the same Congress has decreed and sanctioned the following

FEDERAL CONSTITUTION OF THE UNITED MEXICAN STATES

In the name of GOD, all powerful, author and supreme legislator of society. The general constituent Congress of the Mexican Nation, in the discharge of the duties confided to them by their constituents, in order to establish and fix its political Independence, establish and confirm its Liberty, and promote its prosperity and glory, decree as follows:

CONSTITUTION OF THE UNITED MEXICAN STATES

TITLE 1---Of the Mexican Nation, its Territory and Religion

1. The Mexican Nation is forever free and independent of the Spanish government, and every other power.
2. Its Territory consists of that, which was formerly called the viceroyalty of New Spain, that styled the captain generalship of Tucaton, that of the commandant generalship formerly called the Internal Provinces of East and West, and that of Lower and Upper California, with the lands annexed, and adjacent lands in both seas. By a constitutional law, a demarcation of the limits of the Federation will be made as soon as circumstances will permit.
3. The religion of the Mexican Nation, is, and will be perpetually, the Roman Catholic Apostolic. The Nation will protect it by wise and just laws, and prohibit the exercise of any other whatever.

TITLE 2--- Form of Government of the Nation, of its integral parts and division of Supreme Power

4. The Mexican Nation adopts for its government, the form of Republican representative, popular Federal.
5. The parts of this Federation are the States and Territories as follows: The State of Chiapas, Chiuahua, Coahuila and Texas, Durango, Guanajuato, Mexico, Michoacan, New Leon, Oajaca, Pueblo de los Angeles, Quetaro, Son Luis Potosi, Sinora and Sinaloa, Tobasco, Tumaulipas, Vera Cruz Xalisco, Yucatan Tacatecas; the Territoy of Upper Caliafornia, Lower Caliafornia, Colima and Santa Fe of New Mexico---a constitutional law shall fix the character of Tlaxcala.
6. The supreme power of the Federation will be divided for its exercise, in Legislative, Executive, and Judicial.

TITLE 3 SECTION 1st—Legislative Power, of its nature and the mode of exercising it

7. The legislative power of the Federation, shall be disposed in a General Congress, this to be divided in two houses, one of Deputies (Representatives) and the other of Senators.

SECTION 2nd---Of the House of Representatives.

8. The House of Representatives shall be composed of Representatives elected totally every two years, by the citizens of the States.

9. The qualifications of the electors shall be constitutionally prescribed by the Legislatures of the States, to whom, likewise, appertains the regulation of the elections, in conformity with the principles established by this Constitution

10. The general basis for the appointment of representatives, shall be the population.

11. For every 80,000 souls, one representative shall be appointed, or for a fraction which passes 40,000. The State which may not contain this population, shall, notwithstanding, appoint one representative.

12. A consensus of the whole Federation, which shall be formed in five years and renewed every ten, shall serve to designate the number of Deputies corresponding to each State; and in the mean time, it shall be regulated agreeably to the basis established in the former Article, by the census which governed in the election of Deputies in the present Congress.

13. In the same manner shall be elected in each State, the necessary number of supernumerary representatives, in the ratio of one for every three full representatives, or for a fraction amounting to two; the states which may contain less than three full representatives shall elect one supernumerary.

14. The Territory which may contain more than 40,000 inhabitants shall appoint a full representative and one supernumerary, who shall have a voice and vote in the formation of laws and decrees.

15. The Territory which may not contain the foregoing number of population, shall appoint one full representative and one supernumerary, who shall be entitled to a voice in all matters. The election of representatives for the Territories shall be regulated by a special law.

16. In every State and Territory of the Federation, the appointment Of Representatives shall be made on the first Sunday in October previous to its renovation. The election to be indirect.

17. The election of representatives concluded, the electoral college shall remit through their President to the Council of Government, a legal return of the election, and notify the elected of their appointment by an official letter, which shall serve as a credential of election.

18. The president of the Council of Government shall give to the returns, referred to in the preceding Article, the direction prescribed by the regulations of said Council.

19. To be a Representative it is required---First, to be at the time of the election. Twenty-five years of age complete. Second, to have been a resident of the State, from which elected, at least two years, or be born in the State, although a resident in another.

20. Those not born in the territory of the Mexican Nation, to be representatives, must have, besides eight years' residence in it, 8000 dollars of real estate in any part of the Republic, or an occupation that produces them 1000 per year.

21. Exceptions to the foregoing Article---First, Those born in any other part of America, that in 1810 appertained to Spain, and has not united itself to another nation, nor remains subject to a former, to whom three years' residence in the Territory of the Federation is sufficient, in addition to the requisite prescribed in the 19th Article. Second, The military not born in the Territory of the republic, who, with arms, sustained the independence of the country, eight years.

APPENDIX B
ROSTER OF JUAN SEGUIN'S COMPANY AT
SIEGE OF BEXAR (with original sequence and spelling)

"Office of the Commissioner of Claims, February 10, 1858
List of the individuals of the volunteer company of the municipality of
Bexar who participated in the taking of this city of Bexar:

Captain: Juan N. Seguin
1st Lieutenant: Placido Benavides
2nd Lieutenant: Salvador Flores
Sergeant: Manuel Flores
Soldiers
Mateo Cacillas
Ciriaco Conti
Estivan Villareal
Ramon Rubio
Antonio Ruiz
Toribio Herrera
Jose Zuniga
Esmirigildo Ruiz
Ygnacio Espinosa
Vicente Ramos
Pablo Cacillas
Juan Jose Palacios
Paulin de la Garza

Julian Conti
Carlos Chacon
Domingo Diaz
Jesus Garcia
Agapito Cervantes
Clemente Bustillo
Luis Castanon
Francisco Diaz
Pablo Mansolo
Eduardo Hernandez
Agapito Tejada
Vincente Zepeda
Juan Jose Arrocha
Jesus Gomez
Margil Salinas
Miguel Cilva
Manuel Escalera
Francisco Gomez
Francisco Salinas
Jose Maria de la Garza
Francisco Valdez
Antonio Hernandez
Fernando Curvier
Clemente Garcia
Miguel Mata
Nepomuceno Navarro
Ambrosio Rodriguez
Jose Alemeda
Domingo Losoyo
Pedro Herrera
Pablo Salinas
Guadalupe Garcia
Pedro Gaona
Manuel Bueno
Francisco Miranda
Juan Gimenes
Marcelino de la Garza
Manuel Gallardo

Eduardo Ramires
Graviel(sic) Gonzales
Gregorio Hernandez

(I,) Juan N. Seguin, Captain of the volunteer company of the municipality of Bexar,

Certify that the individuals who appear on the preceding list are the same as those I listed for (fragment)."

Source: Jesus F. de la Pena, A Revolution Remembered.

APPENDIX C
TEXAS DECLARATION OF INDEPENDENCE
(with original spelling)

The Unanimous Declaration of Independence made by the Delegates of the People of Texas in General Convention at the town of Washington on the 2nd day of March 1836,

When a government has ceased to protect the lives, liberty and property of the people, from whom its legitimate powers are derived, and for the advancement of whose happiness it was instituted, and so far from being a guarantee for the enjoyment of those inestimable and inalienable rights, becomes an instrument in the hands of evil rulers for their oppression,

When the Federal Republican Constitution of their country, which they have sworn to support, no longer has a substantial existence, and the whole nature of their government has been forcibly changed, without their consent, from a restricted federative republic, composed of sovereign states, to a consolidated central military despotism, in which every interest is disregarded but that of the army and the priesthood, both the eternal enemies of civil liberty, the ever ready minions of power, and the usual instruments of tyrants,

When long after the spirit of the constitution has departed, moderation is at length so far lost by those in power, that even the semblance of freedom is removed, and the forms themselves of the constitution discontinued and so far from their petitions and remonstrances being regarded, the agents who bear them are thrown into dungeons, and mercenary armies sent forth to force a new government upon them at the point of a bayonet,

When, in consequence of such acts of malfeasance and abdication on the part of the government, anarchy prevails, and civil society is dissolved into its original elements, In such a crisis, the first law of nature, the right of self-preservation, the inherent and inalienable rights of the people to appeal to first principles, and to take their political affairs into their own hands in extreme cases, enjoins it as a right towards themselves, and a sacred obligation to their posterity, to abolish such government, and create another in its stead, calculated to rescue them from impending dangers, and to secure their future welfare and happiness,

Nations, as well as individuals, are amenable for their acts to the public opinion of mankind, A statement of a part of our grievances is therefore submitted to an impartial world, in justification of the hazardous but unavoidable step now taken, of severing our political connection with the Mexican people, an assuming an independent attitude among the nations of the earth,

The Mexican government, by its colonization laws, invited and induced the Anglo-American population of Texas to colonize its wilderness under the pledged faith of a written constitution, that they should continue to enjoy that constitutional liberty and republican government to which they had been habituated in the land of their birth, the United States of America,

In this expectation they have been cruelly disappointed, inasmuch as the Mexican nation has acquiesced in the late changes made in the government by General Antonio Lopez de Santa Anna, who, having overturned the constitution of his country, now offers us the cruel alternative, either to abandon our homes, acquired by so many privations, or submit to the most intolerable of all tyranny, the combined despotism of the sword and the priesthood,

It has sacrificed our welfare to the state of Coahuila, by which our interests have been continually depressed through a jealous and partial course of legislation, carried on at a far distant seat of government, by a hostile majority, in an unknown tongue, and this too, notwithstanding we have petitioned in the humblest terms for the establishment of a separate state government, and have, in accordance with the provisions of the national constitution, presented to the general Congress a republican constitution, which was, without just cause, contemptuously rejected,

It incarcerated in a dungeon, for a long time, one of our citizens, for no other cause but a zealous endeavor to procure the acceptance of our constitution, and the establishment of a state government,

It has failed and refused to secure, on a firm basis, the right of trial by jury, that palladium of civil liberty, and the only safe guarantee for the life, liberty, and property of the citizen,

It has failed to establish any public system of education, although possessed of almost boundless resources, (the public domain,) and although it is an axiom in political science, that unless a people are educated and enlightened, it is idle to expect the continuance of civil liberty, or the capacity for self government,

It has suffered the military commandants, stationed among us, to exercise arbitrary acts of oppression and tyranny, thus trampling upon the most sacred rights of the citizens, and rendering the military superior to the civil power,

It has dissolved, by force of arms, the state Congress of Coahuila and Texas, and obliged our representatives to fly for their lives from the seat of government, thus depriving us of the fundamental political right of representation,

It has demanded the surrender of a number of our citizens, and ordered military detachments to seize and carry them into the Interior for trial, in contempt of the civil authorities, and in defiance of the laws and of the constitution,

It has made piratical attacks upon our commerce, by commissioning foreign desperadoes, and authorizing them to seize our vessels, and to convey the property of our citizens to far distant ports for confiscation,

It denies us the right of worshipping the Almighty according to the dictates of our own conscience, by the support of a national religion, calculated to promote the temporal interest of human functionaries, rather than the glory of the true and living God,

It has demanded us to deliver up our arms, which are essential to our defence, the rightful property of freemen, and formidable only to tyrannical governments,

It has invaded our country both by sea and by land, with intent to lay waste our territory, and drive us from our homes; and has now a large mercenary army advancing, to carry on against us a war of extermination,

It has, through its emissaries, incited the merciless savage, with the tomahawk and scalping knife, to massacre the inhabitants of our defenseless frontiers,

It hath been, during the whole time of our connection with it, the contemptible sport and victim of successive military revolutions, and hath continually exhibited every characteristic of a weak, corrupt, and tyrannical government,

These, and other grievances, were patiently borne by the people of Texas, untill they reached that point at which forebearance ceases to be a virtue, We then took up arms in defence of the national constitution, We appealed to our Mexican brethren for assistance, Our appeal has been made in vain, Though months have elapsed, no sympathetic response has yet been heard from the interior, We are, therefore, forced to the melancholy conclusion that the Mexican people have acquiesced in the destruction of their liberty, and the substitution therefor of a military government; that they are unfit to be free, and incapable of self government,

The necessity of self-preservation, therefore, now decrees our eternal political separation,

We, therefore, the delegates with plenary powers of the people of Texas, in solemn convention assembled, appealing to a candid world for the necessities of our condition, do hereby resolve and declare, that our political connection with the Mexican nation has forever ended, and that the people of Texas do now constitute a free, Sovereign, and independent republic, and are fully invested with all the rights and attributes which properly belong to independent nations, and, conscious of the rectitude of our intentions, we fearlessly and confidently commit the issue to the decision of the Supreme arbiter of the destinies of nations.

(Note: among the signatures appearing on this Declaration of Independence are the following in original spelling: Francis Ruiz, J. Antonio Navarro and Lorenzo de Zavala)

APPENDIX D
MUSTER ROLL OF SEGUIN'S COMPANY AT
SAN JACINTO (with original sequence and spelling)

NAME & RANK

Irvin N. Seguin--Captain
Manuel Flores--1st Sergt
Antonio Manchaca--2nd (Sergeant)
Neph Flores--1st Corpl
Ambro Rodengues--2nd (Corporal)
Antonio Cruz
Jose Maria Mocha
Edwardo Ramarez
Lucio Enniques
Matias Curvier
Antonio Curvier
Simon Ariola
Manl. Avoca
Pedro Herrera
Manl. Turin
Thos. Maldona
Cesario Carmona (Carnonia)
Jacinto Pena
N. Navarro
Andres Varcenas

(Note: Juan Lopez, who informally joined the company during the fording of Buffalo Bayou is not listed on the above official muster roll. Lopez was the only member of Seguin's company to be wounded at the battle of San Jacinto.)

Source: Jesus F. de la Pena, A Revolution Remembered

APPENDIX E
BIOGRAPHICAL SKETCHES OF SOME TEJANOS/TEJANAS

Abamillo, Juan: Sergeant. Born in Bexar, date unknown. He initially served as a private in the company of Captain Juan N. Seguin. Initially entered the Alamo on February 23 where he was killed in action during Santa Anna's assault March 6 1836.

Abrego, Gaspar Flores de: Born in San Antonio de Bexar January 5, 1781, son of Vicente Flores and Maria Antonia de las Fuentes Fernandez. Gaspar was elected alcalde of San Antonio four times. He, along with Juan Seguin and others, initiated the first revolutionary convention, asking all Texans to join him in October 1834 to discuss the dictatorial actions being taken by Mexican President Antonio Lopez de Santa Anna. Gaspar provided early volunteers holding the Alamo with food and provisions. He was elected a Bexar representative to the Convention of 1836 but did not attend. Leading his family to safety in East Texas, he died near San Felipe, probably of fever, September 6, 1836. His four sons were prominent in the Texas revolution. They were Salvador, Manuel N., Nepomuceno and Jose Maria Flores.

Alavez, Francisca: Date and place of birth are unknown. She was reportedly the common-law wife of Captain Telesforo Alavez, a member of General Urrea's Cuautla cavalry regiment of which he was the paymaster. Attractive, outspoken and brave, Senora Alavez, the

"Angel of Goliad," saved many insurgent prisoners taken by General Urrea at Goliad and other locations from execution. Other last names attributed to her are Alvarez, Alavesco, Alevesco and Alavesque. She was also called Francita, Panchita and Pancleta. When she and her husband eventually returned to Mexico City, he may have abandoned her. Later she lived in Matamoros, then moved to Texas where she and her descendants lived and worked on the Cortina, later the King ranch. Many Texans, aware of her heroism during the revolution, contributed to her welfare. Her date of death is unknown. She was reportedly buried in an unmarked grave on the ranch. A handsome statue and plaque honoring her are outside the walls of La Bahia, the presidio of Goliad.

Aldrete, Jose Miguel: His last name is also spelled Alderete. Born in 1810 at La Bahia, he was the alcalde there from 1823-24. A supporter of the revolution, he fought at the siege and assault at Bexar in the company of Placido Benavides. At Goliad/La Bahia with Philip Dimitt (or Dimmitt) he was one of the signers of the Goliad Declaration of Independence. He provided many cattle and provisions to the Texas army. He married Candelaria, a daughter of the famous de Leon family. Aldrete was elected judge of Refugio County, Texas, serving there from 1841-44. In 1848 he lived in Corpus Christi. He was initially buried in 1858 in Refugio but later reburied by his son, Trinidad, in 1874 in Villa Nueva de Camargo, Tamaulipas, Mexico. Family members still reside in the latter as well as Rio Grande City, Texas.

Alsbury, Juana Navarro: Born in Bexar and baptized December 28, 1812. Her father was Jose Angel Navarro and her uncle was Juan Antonio Navarro, who signed the Texas Declaration of Independence. She was a niece of Juan Martin de Veramendi, once the Texas governor, and she was a cousin by marriage to the famous Jim Bowie. Bowie fell ill during the siege of the Alamo and Mrs. Alsbury, wife of Doctor Horace Alsbury who was away warning Houston of the Alamo's dismal situation, nursed Bowie in the Alamo until his death during the Mexican assault. She served as the unsuccessful emissary to Santa Anna on Travis' behalf the night before the assault. Doctor Alsbury later was captured by General Adrian Woll and imprisoned in Mexico until 1844. At his death Juana remarried Juan Perez, a cousin of her first husband. She died July 23, 1888 at her son's home on the Salado Creek.

Arocha, Antonio Cruz y (also called Antonio Cruz): Born in Mexico and grew up in Tejas. He was a private in Juan Seguin's company and with Seguin, his cousin, left the Alamo on the night of February 29, 1836 to secure assistance from Fannin at Goliad. They rode through the encircling Mexican positions to deliver Travis' plea but were told that Fannin was already on the march to relieve the Alamo. Antonio and Seguin made their way to Gonzales where they joined Houston's army, then provided the rear guard for Houston during his retreat across East Texas to San Jacinto. Arocha fought at San Jacinto where he was muster roll listed as Antonio Cruz. Later enlisted as a sergeant in Company B, commanded by Captain Manuel Flores. Date and place of death are unknown.

Arocha, Jose Maria: Born in Tejas and enlisted in the Seguin company October 11, 1836. Fought at the battle for Bexar, where he was muster roll listed as Juan Jose Arrocha. He was discharged from the army November 4, 1836, the same year he sold the land earned from his military service. Arocha died at San Antonio in 1841.

Arocha, Manuel: Date and place of birth are unknown. He was a member of the Seguin company organized at Gonzales after the fall of the Alamo. His name was listed as "Manl. Avoca" on the muster roll of Seguin's company at San Jacinto, earning him 640 acres for that service. Date and place of death are not known.

Arreola, Simon: Born in Bexar, date unknown. His last name was also spelled Ariola, as listed on the muster roll of Seguin's company at the battle of San Jacinto. Joined the Seguin company February 23, 1836 and discharged from the army at Nacogdoches, July 31, 1836. Date and place of death are unknown.

Badillo, Juan Antonio: Born in Tejas and resident of Bexar. Badillo served as a sergeant with Juan Seguin whom he accompanied to the Alamo in February. Killed in action at the Alamo March 6 1836.

Barcines, Andres: Born in Bexar. His last name also spelled Barcenas, A member of Seguin's company he and Anselmo Bergara were detailed by Seguin to reconnoiter the Alamo vicinity during its siege. At the completion of their mission Barcines and Bergara reported to Houston at Gonzales they had heard the Alamo had fallen and all its defenders executed. Houston, fearing this disastrous news would demoralize the army he was assembling, had the two men arrested and sequestered as spies. Barcines appears on the Seguin company muster roll at San Jacinto as Andres Varcenas. He was also a member of Company B of Seguin's later regiment, appearing on that roster as Andrew Barcenas. Died in San Antonio in 1839. Colonel Seguin was the administrator of his estate, May 27, 1839.

Benavides, Placido: Born in Reynosa, Tamaulipas, Mexico, in 1810. Went to Texas in 1828 to become secretary to Fernando de Leon, son of empresario Martin de Leon. Married to Augustina de Leon, daughter of Martin, in 1832, the same year he was elected alcalde of Guadalupe Victoria. Established a ranch on Zorillo Creek, renamed Placido (later corrupted to Placedo) Creek. Reelected alcalde of Guadalupe Victoria in 1834. He was a famous revolutionary who led his fellow Victorianos against frequent Indian attacks and also commanded a company of thirty Tejanos capturing La Bahia at Goliad on October 10, 1835. On October 14 he led his company to Bexar to join General Austin in the siege and assault on General Cos' occupying force, resulting in the latter's surrender of San Antonio and withdrawal toward Mexico. Lieutenant Benavides and his company also served with Doctor James Grant when Grant's force was decimated by General Urrea at Agua Dulce. Benavides warned Grant that more than sixty Mexican dragoons were surrounding their column of volunteers and horse herd. He wanted to fight but Grant ordered him to carry the warning to Fannin at Goliad that Urrea was nearby. Riding hard, Benavides spread the word to settlers all the way to Victoria of the approaching Mexicans. This effort earned him the sobriquet "Paul Revere of the Texas Revolution." Another, but unheeded, warning from Benavides went to Travis at the Alamo, informing the latter that Santa Anna's army was crossing the Rio Grande River in strength. Travis was not duly concerned at the time. A supporter of the Constitution of 1824, Benavides preferred that Texas be a separate state within the Mexican federation rather than an independent nation. Discouraged by his friends' desire for independence and their animosity, Benavides retired to his Victoria ranch yet couldn't escape the conflict. He discovered a seriously wounded and exhausted Isaac D. Hamilton of the Alabama Red Rovers escaping from Goliad. He placed Hamilton in his wagon to care for him at his ranch but Mexican cavalry intercepted them. Benavides' choices were to be taken prisoner with Hamilton or surrender Hamilton. He chose the latter. Taken to Goliad, Hamilton was later aided in escaping by none other than the Angel of Goliad, Panchita Alavez. Captain Benavides and family found themselves persecuted by former comrades and friends after the war. The hatred was so intense that Benavides was ordered into exile (and safety) in Louisiana with the de Leons. Placido died of an unknown cause in Opelousas in 1837 at the early age of 27 years. His widow died five years later in Tamaulipas, Mexico, where she had fled with her mother, Patricia de Leon. The city of Benavides in Duval County was founded by and named for Placido's namesake nephew, hardly compensation for the contributions and suffering of Placido and his family. Placido's brothers later returned to Texas to reclaim what lands and property they could. Benavides descendants still reside in the Mission Valley and Rio Grande City areas of Texas. A possible Benavides descendent, Army Master Sergeant Roy P. Benavidez earned the Congressional Medal of Honor, the highest military decoration of the United States, for valor in combat in VietNam.

Bergara, Anselmo: Place and date of birth are unknown. He and Andres Barcines were the two Tejanos Juan Seguin sent scouting to ascertain the status of the Alamo and its defenders. Later the two reported to Houston at Gonsalez that the Alamo had fallen, all its defenders slain and their corpses burned. Bergara appears on Seguin's regimental roll in Captain Manuel Flores' Company B. Place and date of death are unknown.

Carbajal, Jose Maria Jesus: Born in Bexar, date unknown. Traveled to the United States in 1823 and returned to Tejas to become the surveyor of the Martin de Leon colony. He planned the layout of Guadalupe Victoria (present day Victoria, Texas) and married a de Leon daughter, Maria del Refugio de Leon Garza. Because of his federalist sympathies and activities in the legislature of the State of Coahuila y Tejas, he was sought and arrested for rebellion by Colonel Domingo de Ugartechea, commandant at Bexar. Escaping, Carabajal went to New Orleans and a chartered a vessel to supply Texas volunteers. The vessel capsized and Carbajal was arrested and imprisoned but again escaped. In 1835 he was among the sixty-six volunteers, including Tejanos Padilla, de Leon, and Benavides, who signed an October 9 compact assuring citizens of Guadalupe Victoria that they would protect the citizenry if they supported the provisions of the Constitution of 1824 and individual liberty. Although elected to the Convention of 1836, he did not attend as he was leading his family to safety from Santa Anna. In 1839 he commanded a group of volunteers which defeated a centralist force near Mier, Mexico. There he was wounded. Preferring Texas remain a Mexican, but independent, state, Carbajal commanded a Mexican division in the war with the Unites States in 1846. He became governor of the Mexican states of Tamaulipas and San Luis Potosi. He died in Tamaulipas in 1874.

Cassiano, Jose: Born in San Remo, Italy in 1791 and emigrated to Tejas where he married Josepha Menchaca, daughter of Jose Menchaca. Cassiano settled in San Antonio where he became a prosperous and well-known merchant. He generously gave food and supplies to the Texas army, even warned Travis that Santa Anna's army of some 3,000 troops had arrived in Saltillo, Mexico. With Blas Herrera, he also reported that Santa Anna's army of approximately six thousand was crossing the Rio Grande and heading toward San Antonio de Bexar. Cassiano died in his Dolorosa Street home in San Antonio January 1, 1862

Cubiere, Antonio: Date and place of birth are not known, nor are his place and date of death. He was a member of Captain Juan Seguin's company at the battle of San Jacinto.

Cubiere, Cesario: Born in Bexar and enlisted in Lieutenant Manuel Flores' company November 5, 1836. However, his name does not appear on the muster roll of that unit. He was discharged February 3, 1838. Died in Bexar in 1841.

Cubiere, Fernando: Date and place of birth are unknown, as are the date and place of his death A member of Seguin's company at the siege and attack of Bexar which forced the surrender and retreat of General Cos from San Antonio.

Cubiere, Matias: Born in Bexar in 1814. Served with Seguin at San Jacinto, where he was muster-listed as Mathias Curvier. Enlisted in Lieutenant Manuel Flores' Company B as the 3rd Sergeant. Married Irulella Garza November 11, 1837. He was a member of the Texas Veterans Association and died in San Antonio in 1877.

Enriquez, Lucio: Born in San Antonio, date unknown. Served in Seguin's company from March 5 to June 5, 1836. In the San Jacinto muster roll he was listed as Lucio Enniques. After San Jacinto he enlisted in Lieutenant Manuel Flores' company, enrolled as 2nd Sergeant Lucio Ernigue. Received a total of 960 acres of land in recognition of his services to Texas. May have died in 1852 after which his widow sold his acreage.

Escalera, Manuel: Date and place of birth are unknown. He served in the Seguin volunteer company during the siege and assault on Bexar. The three Escaleras--Manuel, Juan and Jose Maria--provided invaluable scouting reports to Captain Philip Dimitt while he was in command of the Goliad/La Bahia garrison.

Espalier, Carlos. Private. Born in Bexar in 1819 and was a member of Placido Benavides' company at the battle for Goliad. He left the Alamo in early February 1836, but returned in early March with Crockett. The seventeen-year old Espalier assisted Bowie on his sick bed in the Alamo and was killed nearby during the final assault. His aunt received compensation for her nephew's service to Texas.

Esparza, Ana Salazar de: Wife of Gregorio Esparza who tended a small cannon at the Alamo until he was killed during the assault. She was born in San Antonio around 1806 and baptized January 23, 1813. Gregorio was her second marriage after the death of her first husband in 1825. Senora Esparza had four children. Son Enrique recalled the assault inside the Alamo: soldiers firing into the room where he hid, their killing another boy standing beside Enrique, even their burning of the defenders' corpses. Senora Esparza and children were interned in the home of Ramon Musquiz and interrogated by Santa Anna. Later she moved to Pleasanton, Texas. She died December 12, 1847.

Esparza Gregorio: Born and resident of Bexar, Esparza was killed in the Alamo while manning his small cannon. He fought at Bexar under Placido Benavides. Gregorio gathered his family and they entered the Alamo through a window due to the sudden, unexpected arrival of Santa Anna's army. "My father's body was lying near the cannon he tended," remembered his son, Enrique. Gregorio's brother, Francisco, a centralist soldier during the battle for Bexar, appealed to General Cos for the body of his brother, which was granted. Gregorio Esparza was the only Alamo defender not burned in the Alamo pyre but buried in what is today the Ben Milam Square in San Antonio.

Flores, Manuel N.: Born in Bexar and served as Sergeant in Seguin's volunteer company at Bexar, later as 1st Sergeant of Seguin's I Company at San Jacinto. He was the brother-in-law of Seguin. Later Flores became the lieutenant commanding Company B of the Seguin regiment. While first sergeant at the battle of San Jacinto, Flores yelled at his men to get up and pursue the Mexicans. "Get up you cowards! Santa Anna's men are running!" Manuel Flores advocated the Constitution of 1824 and preferred that Texas become an independent state within the Mexican nation, rather than break away from Mexico as an independent republic. In 1838 he and his wife established a ranch on the south side of the Guadalupe River near Seguin, Texas. Manuel Flores again came to Texas' defense by joining a group of volunteers pursuing Mexican General Raphael Vasquez after the latter's surprise occupation of San Antonio in 1842. Date and place of death are unknown. Descendents of the Flores family donated the land upon which Floresville, Wilson County, was established.

Flores, Jose Maria: He was born in San Antonio in 1808. Served in his brother Manuel's Company B of the Seguin regiment from January 15 to June 10, 1836. Died in San Antonio December 3, 1868.

Flores Nepomuceno: Born in Bexar in 1811. His father was Jose Gaspar Flores de Abrego and his brother was Manuel Flores. His sister was the wife of Juan Seguin. Flores was 1st Corporal in Seguin's Company I at San Jacinto. Died December 2, 1878.

Flores, Salvador: Born in Bexar, perhaps in 1806. Married Maria Flores May 24, 1841 and fathered five children. Later married Concepcion Rojo on September 30, 1848. They had two children. On October 2, 1835 Salvador Flores held a meeting of local ranchers who supported the revolution. Salvador led a force of volunteers skirmishing with the Mexicans on Salado Creek in mid-October, earning him a commendation from General Stephen F. Austin. Lieutenant Salvador Flores was ordered to scout the four Catholic missions immediately south and southwest of San Antonio along with Jim Bowie. He, his men and Bowie fought in the battle of the Concepcion Mission October 28, 1835. Aware of the superb horsemanship of Flores' men, Austin ordered Flores' unit to reconnoiter Mexican troop movements between the Nueces and Medina Rivers plus burn anything of value to the advancing Mexicans. Flores' company took part in the Grass (Zacate) fight with a Mexican army pack train on November 26, 1835. Next, Salvador was the 2nd Lieutenant in Captain Seguin's company at the siege and assault on Bexar, driving out General Martin Perfecto de Cos and his superior force. Salvador Flores' next mission was to protect families on the southern ranches from depredations from the retreating Mexican troops and hostile Indians. Commissioned a captain January 14, 1836 he volunteered to monitor Mexican troop movements in the Laredo area. During the siege of the Alamo, Salvador commanded the artillery and left the old mission probably following the departure of Juan Seguin and Antonio Cruz Arocha. During the Runaway Scrape, Salvador and his company protected fleeing families from the lower ranches. Salvador was the captain commanding Company C of the Seguin regiment in late 1836. In 1837 he was assigned to the Texas 1st Cavalry Regiment and served in several companies fighting hostile Indians. In 1842 he was again called upon to organize and command 100 Tejanos to counter the surprise invasion of San Antonio by Mexican forces under General Adrian Woll.

Fuentes, Antonio: Corporal. He was born and a resident of Bexar, joining the Seguin company as a private during the battle for Bexar, December 5-10, 1835. Remained in the Alamo after Seguin and Antonio Cruz left to relay Travis' urgent need for reinforcements to Fannin at Goliad. Fuentes fell at the Alamo during the Mexican assault.

Fuqua, Benjamin. Benjamin, uncle of Galba who fell at the Alamo, was one of the "Old Original Gonzales 18" who defied the 100-150 Mexican dragoons attempting to capture and remove the small Gonzales cannon September 29, 1835. Earlier Benjamin settled in the Austin colony in 1828, then moved to the Dewitt colony in 1830. There he received, as a single man, one quarter of a league of land to homestead. He was elected a delegate to the Third Texas Consultation in November 1835. As such he was a signer of the "Declaration of the People of Texas" pledging to fight to uphold the Mexican Constitution of 1824 and separate Tejas from Coahuila, yet remain in the Mexican federation. He was the proprietor of a Gonzales establishment called "Luna" which may have been a saloon ,a general mercantile store or both. Later he married Nancy, the daughter of John King.

Fuqua, Galba: Private Fuqua was born in Alabama March 9, 1819 and his family migrated to Tejas. The Fuquas settled in DeWitt colony on May 11, 1830. Galba enrolled in the Gonzales Ranging Company of Mounted volunteers in February 1836. He was one of the thirty-two Gonzales volunteers who entered the Alamo at a gallop after Mexican forces had surrounded the old mission. He was killed in action there at the age of sixteen, the youngest Tejano casualty of the Alamo. Another Fuqua, Galba's uncle Benjamin, was one of the eighteen Gonzales men who initially faced down the Mexican force ordered to retrieve the Gonzales cannon.

Guerrero, Jose Maria (Brigido): Nicknamed "Old, one-eyed Guerreo", he was a private, age 43, and born in Laredo. Sometime during the battle of the Alamo, he locked himself in a cell and claimed to be a prisoner of the insurgents. His life was spared and he was allowed to walk out of the devastated Alamo.

Herrera, Blas Maria: Born in San Antonio February 2, 1802. He married Maria Antonia Ruiz, daughter of Francisco Ruiz, February 3, 1828. The couple had ten children. Served in his cousin, Juan Seguin's, company during the assault of Bexar December 5-10, 1835 although his name is not on the muster roll. He was dispatched by Seguin to report on Mexican troop movements around Laredo. In mid-February, Herrera reported that Santa Anna's army was crossing the Rio Grande River. Seguin next asked Herrera to safely escort the two Bexar representatives, Jose Antonio Navarro and Jose Francisco Ruiz, to the Convention meeting at Washington-on-the-Brazos. There the two Tejanos were among the signers of the Texas Declaration of Independence March 3, 1836. Herrera's scouting skills aided Houston prior to and during the battle of San Jacinto. Herrera was the messenger selected by Juan Seguin, then commanding Bexar, to appeal General Felix Huston's 1836 order to destroy San Antonio. Sam Houston ordered Huston to revoke his order and San Antonio was spared. After the war his family lived in southern Bexar county, near present-day Somerset, Texas. He died July 9, 1878 and was buried in the Ruiz-Herrera cemetery.

Herrera, Pedro: Born in Villa de San Fernando October 15,1806. In 1830 he was a private in the cavalry troop "Alamo de Parras" commanded by Lieutenant Colonel Jose F. Ruiz and which he deserted in August 1831. Participated in the storming of Bexar in December 1835 as a member of Seguin's volunteer company. He further served with Seguin, enlisting February 26, 1836, and served at the battle of San Jacinto. On November 5 he reenlisted in Manuel Flores' Company B, from which he was discharged as the 4th Sergeant in February 1838. He died sometime after 1853.

Leon, Martin de: Born 1765 in Tamaulipas to an old aristocratic Spanish family. Married Patricia de la Garza in 1795 and began ranching in the state of Tamaulipas, Mexico. After a visit to Tejas they moved there, establishing several ranches, the last of which was near San Patricio in 1809. In 1824 he petitioned the newly-established Mexican government to allow him to establish a colony on the lower Guadalupe River. Empresario de Leon moved forty-one families from Tamaulipas to his colony and established the town of Nuestra Senora Guadalupe de Jesus Victoria. His ranch encompassed over 22,000 acres in present-day Victoria County. His famous sons-in-law included Carbajal and Benavides. Martin de Leon died of cholera following the 1833 epidemic and his son Fernando became head of the de Leon family.

Leon, Patricia de la Garza de: Born in Soto de Marina, Tamaulipas in 1775. She and husband Martin had ten children. The family moved to Tejas in 1805 and established several ranches prior to Martin's being granted empresario authority to establish a colony on the Guadalupe River. They developed the town of Guadalupe Victoria, named for the first president of Mexico. She established the first school there as well as a church. The de Leons aided the Texas revolutionaries by smuggling arms and ammunition from New Orleans. Despite the contributions of the entire de Leon family to Texas, they were ostracized and threatened. For safety they fled to Louisiana, later returned to Tamaulipas where she was born. Senora de Leon returned to Texas in 1844 to reclaim some of the possessions stolen from her family after San Jacinto. She died in Victoria in 1849.

Losoyo, Toribio Domingo: Born in Bexar in 1808. Initially a soldier in the Mexican army, he deserted and joined the company of Captain Juan Seguin as a private during the siege of Bexar, 5-10 December 1835. Entered the Alamo with Seguin on February 3, 1836, and departed prior to the final assault. Initially he was thought to have died during the assault on the Alamo. He was discharged October 25, 1836.

Melton, Juana Losoya: Date and place of birth are unknown. She was the wife of Lieutenant Eliel Melton, quartermmaster in the Alamo, where he was killed. Senora Melton's brother, Jose Toribio Losoya was also among the Alamo's defenders but left prior to the final assault. She was one of the women surviving that ordeal. Her date and place of death are unknown.

Menchaca, Antonio: Born in Bexar in 1800. At age eight he was baptized January 17, 1800. He was married to Teresa Ramon in 1826. Menchaca left San Antonio shortly before the battle of the Alamo, then headed east with his family when General Edward Burleson conscripted him into the Texas army. On Juan Seguin's muster roll of his San Jacinto company, Menchaca appears as "Antonio Manchaca, 2nd [Sergeant]." He received an order relayed from Houston by Colonel Sherman at Harrisburg that Seguin's company was to remain behind as guards. He and Seguin went to General Houston to protest the order and were successful. Menchaca procured a meal for the captured Santa Anna after the battle of San Jacinto. A personal friend of Jim Bowie, Menchaca was active in the Texas Veterans' Association. He was elected alderman in San Antonio, also served the city as its mayor pro tem from July 1838 to January 1839. During Mexican General Woll's September 1842 surprise capture of San Antonio and the subsequent battle, Menchaca was wounded in the leg, was captured by Woll's forces but released. He died in San Antonio November 1, 1879 and is buried in the San Fernando cemetery. Continuing the frequent misspelling of his last name, the town of Manchaca, Travis County, was named for him.

Nava, Andres: Born in Bexar in 1810 and served as a private in the Seguin company during the siege and assault of Bexar in December 1835. Entered the Alamo with Seguin and was killed in action during the Mexican assault March 6, 1836.

Navarro, Jose Antonio: Born in Bexar in 1795. Sent to New Orleans for law training at an early age. Along with his uncle, Francisco Ruiz, he advocated independence from Spain. Following the royalist victory at the Battle of the Medina, the bloodiest battle in Texas history, Navarro and Ruiz escaped to Louisiana before returning home after three years. Navarro was the first alcalde of San Antonio de Bexar following Mexican independence from Spain. He was the land commissioner for the DeWitt colony, later was elected to the legislature of the Mexican State of Coahuila y Tejas. In 1835, he declined appointment to the Mexican national senate from Coahuila y Tejas on the advice of his uncle, Francisco Ruiz. On March 3 he signed the 1836 Texas Declaration of Independence developed by the Convention to which he was a Bexar representative along with his uncle, Ruiz, also a signer of the Declaration. In 1844 Navarro was a commissioner representing President Lamar to the disastrous Santa Fe expedition to what is now New Mexico. The expedition was a failure and Navarro was captured, marched to Mexico City, tried and sentenced to be executed for treason. He was offered his life by Santa Anna if he would change his allegiance. His famous reply was "I have sworn to be a Texan and I will not foreswear." During the 1845 revolution deposing Santa Anna, Navarro escaped from prison at Vera Cruz on a steamer bound for Havana. Eventually he made his way to Galveston where he received a hero's reception. He was elected a Bexar representative to the State Constitutional convention, thence to the Texas State Senate where he served three terms. Throughout his career, Navarro advocated equal rights for Tejanos in the legal and political processes of Texas. He was the first Tejano, native-born historian of Texas and supported the secession of Texas in 1861. Four Navarro sons served in the Confederate army. He died in San Antonio in 1870. Navarro County was named for him and its county seat, Corsicana, named as tribute to his Corsican ancestry.

Navarro, Jose Nepomuceno: Born in Bexar in 1811 and served in Seguin's company at the battle of Bexar in December 1835. He was a member of the Texas Veterans' Association and died in San Antonio April 8, 1877.

Padilla, Juan Antonio: Date and place of birth are unknown. Formerly an official of the Spanish government before Mexico's independence, he moved to Texas in 1810. Padilla married but wife's name is unknown. Served as state secretary in the legislature of the State of Coahuila y Tejas and appointed a general land commissioner of the state in 1825. Padilla was among the volunteers joining the Collinsworth force that liberated Victoria and Goliad soon after General Cos' departure for Bexar in October 1835. Among his famous Tejano companions were Sylvestre de Leon, Placido Benavides, and Jose Maria Jesus Carbajal. He also signed the compact written by this group at Guadalupe Victoria October 9 pledging their lives, property and honor to defend its citizens standing "firm to the Republican institutions of the Govt. of Mexico and of Coahuila & Texas under the Constitution of 1824." He was elected a Victoria representative to the Convocation as well as the 1836 Convention but his arrival at Washington-on-the-Brazos was delayed by swollen creeks. Padilla was a member of the General Council, representing Victoria. He died in Houston August 6, 1839 while on a business trip.

Pena, Jacinto: Born in Mexico, date unknown, and grew up in Texas. Joined Seguin's company and fought at San Jacinto. Later he reenlisted in Lieutenant Manuel Flores' Company B and served as the 2nd Corporal. Date and place of death are unknown.

Rodriguez, Ambrosio: Born in Bexar, date unknown. Married to Maria de Jesus Olivarri on January 16, 1828. Joined Juan Seguin's company, serving at Bexar and later at the battle of San Jacinto where he was muster rolled as "Ambro Rodengues, 2nd [Corporal]." Next he served in Manuel Flores' Company B as 2nd Lieutenant Ambrosio Rodigues. Later he also served with Juan Seguin in the 1839 Indian campaign. Died in San Antonio in 1848

Ruiz, Jose Francisco: Born in Bexar January 28, 1783, and was the first schoolmaster of San Antonio in 1803, using his father's house as the school. Elected regidor in 1805 and served as city attorney and several other positions in San Antonio. Fought for Tejas independence from Spain at the battle of Medina on August 18, 1813. Exiled and returned home after Mexico's independence. He was then a member of the militia detachment defeating the short-lived Fredonian rebellion in Nacogdoches, January 1827. Also served as a member of the Mexican Boundary Commission and returned to Bexar as commander of the Alamo de Parras Company. In 1835 he was elected a Bexar representative to the Convention held at Washington-on-the-Brazos in 1836. Along with his nephew, Jose Antonio Navarro, he signed the Texas Declaration of Independence on March 3, 1836. His son, Francisco Antonio Ruiz, was acting alcalde of San Antonio during the siege and battle of the Alamo. Francisco was forced by Santa Anna to identify the bodies of its prominent defenders. The elder Ruiz was elected senator to the First Congress of the Republic of Texas. He died and was buried in San Antonio in 1840.

Seguin, Erasmo (sometimes spelled Erasmus): Born in Bexar in the late 1700s, Erasmo, father of Juan Seguin, held many offices in the Spanish, Mexican and Texas governments. He was postmaster of San Antonio for thirty years and began ranching after 1800. His ranch, La Mora, contained over 22,000 acres and 500 head of cattle. He was loyal to the Spanish king in 1811 when the local garrison mutinied against its

Spanish officers. Despite his support, the Spanish government declared him a traitor based on a letter he had given a revolutionary friend. Seguin's property, including his home, were confiscated and his family turned into the street. He served on the city council until the royalists returned, even leading some fifty soldiers and twenty militiamen to Nacogdoches to reinstate the royalist commander there. By 1818 he had cleared himself of the treason charges and his properties returned. Erasmo was elected alcalde of San Antonio in 1820, again its postmaster in 1822, and then its quartermaster in 1825. He purchased more land for his La Mora ranch and built a well fortified home there as protection against Indian attacks. He was selected by the Coahuila government to notify Moses Austin that his application to establish a colony of 300 families had been approved. When Moses' son, Stephen, came to Texas to assume his dead father's responsibilities as an empresario, Erasmo Seguin was his friend, sponsor and mentor. Their long friendship was personal, practical and political. In 1824, Erasmo was called to Mexico City to participate in the Constitutional Congress establishing the Province of Coahuila y Tejas. Seguin insisted that a proviso be included that a well-developed Tejas later might be granted separate statehood. In August 1835 General Martin Perfecto de Cos arrived in Bexar and relieved Erasmo of his quartermaster duties, even forcing him to walk from San Antonio for threatening to make the general sweep the public square. The elder Seguin provided horses and provisions to Fannin at the battle of Concepcion. Later, Erasmo took his family to East Texas where he remained throughout the revolutionary period. Returning to San Antonio after the war, he found his ranch in ruins. The Republic of Texas paid him $3,000 to compensate for the supplies taken during the war. Despite this ill treatment, Erasmo Seguin remained steadfast to his birthright even serving as a San Antonio magistrate. He died October 30, 1837 at his ranch. Often he was described as "one of the truest friends Texas ever had."

Seguin, Juan Nepomuceno: Born in Bexar in October of 1806, son of Erasmo and a revolutionary hero following the political leadership example of his father. He married Gertrudis Flores de Abrego in January 1826. Juan organized a company of Tejanos joining General Stephen F. Austin's force in the storming of Bexar in December 1835. He led his small company to the Alamo where several of his men died in its defense. Juan was selected by a council of officers within the Alamo to escape the encircled mission and ride to Goliad/La Bahia with Travis' message urgently requesting Fannin reinforcements. Fannin failed to come to Travis' assistance and the Alamo subsequently fell to Santa Anna's assault and all its defenders executed. Seguin gathered a large company of Tejanos at Gonzales and was tasked by General Houston to act as his army's rear guard as Houston retreated eastward during the Runaway Scrape. Meanwhile twenty-five of the Seguin company were placed under Captain Salvador Flores and tasked to assist and protect families from the ranches below Bexar. At the battle of San Jacinto Captain Seguin and his company fought in Colonel Sherman's Second Regiment and distinguished themselves in the defeat of Santa Anna's larger force. As a lieutenant colonel, later colonel, Seguin was the commandant of San Antonio and successfully appealed newly arrived General Felix Huston's order to destroy the city. In February 1837 Seguin and his command were responsible for locating and burying the Alamo defenders' ashes with military honors before withdrawing to Gonzales. Juan returned to Bexar in March 1838 to find he had been elected senator to the Texas Congress. He represented his Bexar constituents as well as all Tejanos by reminding the Congress of Tejano contributions and sacrifices. Despite his own many and varied services to the young republic, Seguin and his family were ridiculed and threatened. Disgusted at this treatment from former friends and comrades, Seguin took his family to Mexico to seek a new and safer life. He wrote, "I feel a foreigner in my own native land." Disillusioned and frustrated, Seguin "sought shelter among those whom I had fought… Thrown into prison in a foreign country, I had no alternatives left but to linger in a loathsome confinement or to accept military service. On the one hand, my wife and children reduced to beggary and separated from me; on the other hand, to turn my arms against my own country." Seguin died in Nuevo Laredo, Mexico, on August 27, 1890. Later his body was moved to the outskirts of the Texas city named for him, Seguin, in Guadalupe County, and re-interred with honors. A statue of Juan Nepomuceno Seguin stands in the Seguin city square.

Tarin, Manuel (also called Manuel Leal): Born in San Antonio on July 24, 1811 and baptized two days later. His father, Vicente Tarin, was an officer in the Alamo de Parras company but left the unit to join Magee's rebellious expedition against the Spanish. After the rebels' defeat at the battle of Medina, Vicente fled to Nacogdoches, leaving his family in San Antonio to fend for itself. Manuel's mother, Juana Isidora Leal, was imprisoned due to her husband's revolutionary activities. The family's property was confiscated and the family was totally dependent upon the charity of the Catholic priest who was Manuel's godfather. Around 1830 Manuel enlisted in the same company his father had deserted, the Alamo de Parras. Unhappy with military life, Manuel deserted twice, was captured both times, nonetheless restored to duty. Assisted Placido Benavides in organizing ranchers to ride to the assistance of Gonzales in October 1835. He became a member of Juan Seguin's company, joining it on February 22, 1836. On the Seguin muster roll at San Jacinto, he was carried as "Manl. Turin." He said he was too ill to fight that day so took no part in the battle of San Jacinto. Seguin handed Tarin's musket to Juan Lopez, the sixteen-year old who informally joined Seguin's unit at Buffalo Bayou prior to the battle. Corporal Manuel Tarin was discharged from the army in July 1837. In 1846 he married Maria Luisa Casares. He died sometime after 1849, probably in San Antonio.

Ximenes, Damacio: Private. He was born in Bexar and fought at Anahuac alongside Travis in the first insurgent battle of the revolution. A member of Seguin's company, Ximenes (also spelled Jimenez) was a cannoneer and helped manhandle the eighteen-pound cannon--the heaviest armament of the Alamo--into place on the old mission's southwest wall. That cannon was fired in answer to Santa Anna's demand for surrender after the latter's army surrounded the Alamo in February. Ximenes probably fired the big cannon. He died manning the eighteen-pounder and defending the Alamo's southwestern corner. Strangely, the family petition for Ximenes' Alamo service remained "undiscovered" in the Bexar County archives until 1986. Hence Damacio Ximenes is the last Tejano recognized for his valor and ultimate sacrifice at the Alamo.

Zavala,Lorenzo de: He was born near Merida, Mexico October 3, 1788. Graduated from the Trindentine Seminary of San Ildefonso in Merida and immediately became embroiled in the political life. He served in numerous positions in the colonial, Spanish and Mexican governments prior to coming to Texas in July 1835. He was imprisoned twice for political activities, once against the Spanish government, again after the ousting of President Guerrero in 1829. Zavala began Yucatan's first newspaper in 1807 and contributed articles throughout his life to that and other periodicals. A prodigious writer, he authored a two-volume history of Mexico as well as a book about his travels in the United States. As a member of the National Congress he aided the drafting of the Constitution of 1824. He was appointed minister to France but resigned due to his growing unrest with the centralist policies of President Santa Anna. Zavala went to Texas and espoused liberty and the Constitution of 1824, which he helped draft. In his words, "I have been President of the general Congress (of Mexico) and my name stands first in the Constitution of Mexico. I have been president in the Senate and today I am a colonist of the Province of Texas." In the absence of Stephen F. Austin, Zavala was a catalyst for reform in Texas, then upon Austin's release from prison, his coadjutor for liberty. Initially he preferred that Texas become an independent (from Coahuila) state within the Mexican federation. When convinced that Santa Anna could not be removed by revolution within Mexico, he eventually opted for an independent Texas. Zavala was a signer of the 1836 Texas Declaration of Independence, along with Ruiz and Navarro. On March 17, 1836, he was unanimously elected the interim Vice President of the Republic of Texas. His home near the San Jacinto battlefield was used as a hospital for the wounded and his son, Major Lorenzo de Zavala, Jr., served as the aide-de-camp of General Houston. Lorenzo de Zavala died November 17, 1836 and was buried on the banks of Buffalo Bayou, which Houston's army previously had forded to reach the battleground of San Jacinto.

APPENDIX F
SOME TEJANOS AND TEJANAS AND THE BATTLES IN WHICH THEY PARTICIPATED

"As a proportion of the population, the active participation of Hispanic native and immigrant residents in the struggle for independence for Texas from Spain and Mexico was equal to or greater in specific battles than that of resident immigrants from the Unites States of the North."

Don Guillermo (not further identified) as quoted in "Hispanic Texian Patriots in the Struggle for Independence."

Anahuac, June 13, 1832:
  Damacio Ximenes

Velasco, June 26, 1832:
  One Tejano, name unknown, killed in action

Gonzales, September 29-October 2, 1835:
  Benjamin Fulqua was one of the "Immortal Gonzales 18" citizens who faced down the Mexican force of 100-150 dragoons from Bexar tasked with returning the small Gonzales cannon to San Antonio on the pretext that it was needed there to bolster defenses. Benjamin's

nephew, Galba, later rode from Gonzales to reinforce Travis' force at the Alamo and died there in its defense on March 6, 1836.

Placido Benavides and twenty-eight neighboring ranchers (for whom no roll is available) responded to Gonzales' pleas for assistance immediately after the battle.

Goliad, October 10, 1835:

Placido Benavides and approximately thirty men (for whom no roll is available) fought in the battle to wrest the La Bahia garrison or presidio from Mexican forces.

Jose Antonio Padilla assisted Benavides in gathering those thirty volunteers. Among the thirty were Jose Miguel Aldrete, Sylvestre de Leon, Jose Maria Jesus Carbajal, and Juan, Jose Maria and Manuel Escalera. Others were Carlos Espalier, Eugenio Benavides, A. Lanstanza, Francisco Garcia, Martin Moran, Francisco de la Portilla, Juan Amador, Marcelino de la Garza and Paulino de la Garza. Also at Goliad were Trinidad Aldrete, A. Constanza, Manuel Escalera, Roberto Galan and Jose Maria de la Garza.

(Primary source: "Hispanic Texian Patriots in the Struggle for Independence")

Salado Creek, mid-October, 1835:

Salvador Flores and Manuel Leal (also called Manuel Tarin) organized forty-one volunteers (for whom no roll is known) who defeated a Mexican force at Salado Creek. Salvador Flores later received a commendation for his actions from General Stephen F. Austin.

Concepcion, October 28, 1835:

Seguin's company, including Salvador Flores, was part of Bowie's scouting party at the San Antonio missions, ending with a battle at Mission Concepcion defeating the Mexican forces from San Antonio sent against them by General Perfecto de Cos. No roll of this volunteer company is known.

The Zacate or Grass Fight, November 26, 1835:

Salvador Flores and his men (for whom there is no known roll) attacked a Mexican supply train enroute to besieged General Cos in

Bexar. Instead of the expected payroll for Cos' troops, Flores discovered forage for livestock.

Bexar, December 5-10, 1835:

Alameda, Jose; Aldrete, Jose M.; Arocha, Jose M.; Badillo, Juan A.; Balli, Antonio; Barbo, Juan J.; Benavides, Placido; Becerra, Jose M.; Berzan, Ansel M.; Bueno, Manuel; Bustillos, Clemente; Cabasos, Albino; Carbajal, Jose J.M.; Carbajal, Mariano; Cardenas, Francisco; Casillas, Juan; Casillas, Mateo; Casillas, Pablo; Castinon, Luis; Cavasos, Albino; Cervantes, Agapito; Chacon, Carlos; Chirino, Jose M.; Cilva (or Cilba), Miguel; Contes, Ciriaco; Contes, Julian; Cruz y Arocha, Antonio; Curbier (or Cuvier), Antonio; Curbier, Fernando; Curvier, Matias; DeLeon, Sylvestre; Diaz, Domingo; Diaz, Francisco; Diaz, Julian; Duran, Blas; Escalera, Manuel; Esparza, Gregorio; Espinosa, Ygnacio; Flores, Manuel; Flores, Salvador; Francois, Sebastian; Fuentes, Antonio; Gallardo, Manuel; Gaona, Pedro; Garcia, Casimiro; Garcia, Clemente; Garcia, Guadalupe; Garcia, Jesus; Garza, Alejando de la; Garza, Ana Maria de la; Garza, Jose Maria de la; Garza, Marcelino de la; Garza, Paulino de la; Gayton, Agapito; Gomez, Francisco; Gomez, Jesus; Gomez, Maximo; Gonzalez, Gabriel (Graviel); Guano, Pedro; Guardo, Manuel; Guerrero, Brigido; Guerreo, Jose M.; Guerreo, Trinidad; Hernandez, Antonio; Hernadez, Eduardo; Hernandez, Gregorio; Herrera, Blas Maria; Herrera, Guadalupe; Herrera, Pedro; Herrera, Toribio; Huizar, Carlos; Jimenez, Juan; Laso, Carlos; Losoya, Jose D.; Losoya, Toribio; Maldonado, Juan; Mancha, Jose; Mancha, Nazario; Mansolo, Pablo; Mata, Miguel; Miranda, Francisco; Mora, Esteban; Nava, Andres; Nava, Antonio; Nava, Pedro; Navarro, Nepomuceno; Palacios, Juan J.; Padilla, Jose A.; Pineda, Jose; Pru, Anselmo; Ramirez, Eduardo; Ramos, Maria Luisa; Ramos, Vicente; Rendon, Jose; Rodriguez, Ambrosio; Rodriguez, Jose de Jesus; Rodriguez, Justo; Rubio, Ramon; Ruiz, Antonio; Ruiz, Esmeraldo; Salinas, Nicholas; Salinas, Frncisco; Salinas, Miguel (Margil); Salinas, Pablo; Seguin, Juan N.; Silva, Manuel (Miguel); Tejado, Agapito; Traviesco, Justo; Valdez, Francisco; Villareal, Esteban; Ybarbo, Jesus; Zepeda, Vicente; Zambrano, Jose; Zambrano, Juan; and Zuniga, Jose.

(Primary source: "Hispanic Texian Patriots in the Struggle for Independence")

The following men were members of the company of Placido Benavides and were recipients of military land grants ("headrights") for their service to Texas: Jose Miguel Aldrete, Jose Maria Arocha, Juan Andres Badillo, Antonio Balli, Juan J.E. Barbo, Juan J.J. Barbo, Jose M. Becerra, Ansel Berzan, Manuel Carbajal, Francisco Cardenas, Juan Casillas, Mateo Casillas, Jose Maria Chirino, Antonio Cruz y Arocha, Antonio Curvier, Matias Curvier, Alejandro de la Garza, Ana Maria de la Garza, Brigido Guerrero, Blas Duran, Antonio Fuentes, Pedro Gaona, Agapito Gayton, Gabriel Gonzalez, Pedro Guano, Jose Maria Guerrero, Trinidad Guerrero, Blas Maria Herrera, Guadalupe Herrera, Carlos Huizar, Toribio Losoya, Juan Maldonado, Jose Maria Mancha, Nazario Mancha, Antonio Nava, Pedro Nava, Jose Pineda, Anselmo Pru, Maria Luisa Ramos, Jose Rendon, Jose de Jesus Rodriguez, Justo Rodriguez, Agapito Tejada, Justo Travieso, Jesus Ybarbo, Jose Zembrano and Juan M. Zembrano.

Others with Benavides were Silvestre de Leon, Carlos Laso, Albino Cavazos, Maximo Gomez, Gregorio Esparza, Francisco Cardenas, Sebastian Francois, Manuel Guardo, Esteban Mora, Jose Antonio Padilla, Nicolas Salinas, Julian Diaz, Manuel Silva and Amado (no last name recorded). The Benavides unit fought under Francis W. Johnson's division during the house-to-house fighting and assault of the tactically significant mansion of Juan Martin Vermamendi in central San Antonio.

Maria Jesus de Garcia. This valiant Tejana, not on any military roster, was officially commended for her bravery in providing water to thirsty insurgents during the Bexar assault. During her efforts to provide water to the troops, she was severely wounded by Mexican soldados firing at her from the Alamo.

San Patricio, February 27, 1836:

Killed in action against Urrea's dragoons were two unnamed Tejanos from Bexar, members of Francis W. Johnson's division.

Wounded during the battle was one Tejano, last name Zembrano, first name unknown, and three others whose names are unknown.

The Alamo, February 22, 1836:

Juan Seguin and nine of his men entered the Alamo on February 3 and remained there while Santa Anna's army was surrounding the mission. Among the Seguin men used as messengers from the Alamo were Juan M. Cabrera, Jacinto Pena, Jose Maria Jimenez and Alejandro de la Garza.

Agua Dulce, March 2, 1836:
Captured and imprisoned in Matamoros as a result of Urrea's ambush of James Grant's command were two Tejanos, one named Cayetano.
Escaped from the ambush and ordered by Dr. Grant to ride to warn Fannin at Goliad was Placido Benavides.

The Fall of the Alamo, March 6, 1836:
Killed in action were Juan Abamillo, Juan Antonio Badillo, Carlos Espalier, Gregorio Esparza, Antonio Fuentes, Galba Fuqua, Andres Nava and Damacio Ximenes.
Taken prisoner but released after he claimed to have been a prisoner of the Texans was Jose Maria (Brigido) Guerrero.
Juan Seguin and his cousin, Jose Arocha Cruz, (also known as Antonio Cruz y Arocha) were selected by a council of Travis' officers to escape the Alamo on the night of February 25-26 to deliver to Fannin at Goliad Travis' plea for reinforcements.
Also escaping the Alamo at about that time were Antonio Menchaca, Toribio Losoya, Salvador Flores, Juan Maria Cabrera, Jose Maria Jimenez and Andres Nava. The latter returned to the old mission with Colonel Crockett in March.

Coleto Creek, March 20, and Goliad, March 27 1836:
Captured and executed Palm Sunday, March 27 were Mariano Carbajal of the San Antonio Greys, Paulino de la Garza and Jose Maria de la Garza, both of Fraser's Militia Company.
Captured but spared from execution was Francisco Garcia of Horton's Rangers.
Although not on any military roster, Francisca Alavez, the "Angel of Goliad" must be recognized for her heroism in preventing the execution of many Texas prisoners of war taken by General Urrea's force at San Patricio, Refugio, Agua Dulce, Copano and Coleto Creek.

San Jacinto April 21, 1836:
(Note: the following names, some misspelled, are as they appear on Seguin's company muster roll.)

Irvin N. Seguin, Captain; Manuel Flores, 1st Sergeant; Antonio Manchaca, 2nd Sergeant ; Neph Flores, 1st Corpl; and Ambro Rodengues, 2nd Corporal

Soldiers: Antonio Cruz, Jose Maria Mocha, Edwardo Ramarez, Lucio Enniques, Matias Curvier, Antonio Curvier, Simon Ariola, Manl. Avoca, Pedro Herrera, Manl. Turin, Thos. Maldona, Cesario Carmona (Carnonia), Jacinto Pena, N. Navarro, and Andres Varcenas. {Note: not appearing on the muster role but present at the battle was Juan Lopez who informally joined the Seguin company at the Buffalo Bayou crossing. Lopez was the only member of the Seguin company who was wounded at San Jacinto. Also not appearing on Seguin's roster but credited with being at San Jacinto were Francisco Salinas, Grabriel Casillas, Jose Maria Jimenez, Jose Malona and Jose Maria Arocha.

Other Tejanos at San Jacinto, not of the Seguin company, were Lorenzo de Zavala, Jr., Houston's aide de camp; Peter Lopez of the Cavalry Company; Martin Flores, musician of the Regular Army's Company A; Antonio Trevino of Company D of the First Regiment of Texas Volunteers; and Jose Molino (his real name was Jose P. Lavina) of Company A, Second Regiment Nacogdoches Volunteers.

Serving at unrecorded locations but discharged from the Seguin company in February, 1842 were the following: Domingo Dias, Antonio Hernandez, Francisco Diaz, Gregorio Hernandez, Luis Castanon, Agapito Cervantes, Pablo Mansolo, Carlos Chacon, Jesus Garcia, Clemente Garcia and Clemente Bustillo.

San Antonio de Bexar, September 11, 1842:
Antonio Menchaca, a former member of Seguin's company at San Jacinto, was among the volunteers responding to the surprise occupation of San Antonio by Mexican General Woll's forces. In the ensuing fight, Menchaca was wounded. Salvador Flores, a member of Seguin's volunteer company of Bexar, was called upon to organize some 100 Tejanos who fought the Woll invasion. The names of these 100 men apparently were not recorded.

APPENDIX G
THE FAMOUS, DISAPPEARING CANNON OF THE REVOLUTION

THE GONZALES "COME AND TAKE IT" CANNON

Possible provenances of this cannon:
1. This small cannon, initially described as a Spanish six-pounder of bronze, was loaned empresario Green DeWitt in 1831 to protect his colony against frequent Indian attacks. He asked for and received permission to be issued the cannon from Ramon Musquiz, Political Chief of Bexar. The cannon may have been one of the many captured at the June 20, 1813 battle of Alazan Creek, just south of Bexar, between the Spanish royalists and republican insurgents. Or
2. The Gonzales cannon was cast in Mexico of iron, not bronze, and mistakenly issued to the DeWitt colony by the Bexar garrison as a six pounder since its outside muzzle diameter approximated the diameter of a six pound ball. In reality it was much smaller weapon.

After the Fredonian uprising, the Mexican commandant of Bexar, Colonel Domingo Ugartechea, decided to ask for the return of the Gonzales cannon on the pretext it was needed for the defense of Bexar. The alcalde of Gonzales, Andrew Ponton, polled the town's citizens and their near-unanimous vote (only three were for surrendering the cannon) was to keep it. To prevent the cannon's being seized by the Mexicans by surprise, it was buried in the Davis peach orchard outside Gonzales. Meanwhile Ugartechea sent a detachment of 100-150 troops under Lieutenant Francisco Castaneda to retrieve the cannon and return it to Bexar.

The defiant Gonzales citizens prepared to meet this threat, dug up the cannon, placed wooden wheels on it and collected black powder and bits of scrap iron to use for ammunition. Volunteers assembled at Gonzales from other communities like San Felipe, Goliad and Victoria. The battle of Gonzales ensued on the morning of October 2, 1835. The Gonzales cannon was fired at the Mexicans who, after a brief skirmish, retired back to Bexar with one or two casualties, leaving behind the cannon they had sought.

There are at least two versions of what later happened to the Gonzales cannon, now a symbol of Texas liberty and depicted upon the white and black flag stitched by Sarah DeWitt (Green's wife) and other ladies on a wedding dress the night before the battle.

Version 1. Blacksmith Noah Smith maintained that after the battle of Gonzales the cannon was being hauled to Bexar October 14 to reinforce the liberty-minded insurgents gathering at the Alamo. The wheel axles of the cannon began smoking a few miles outside of Gonzales and the cannon, minus its burning wheels, was buried next to Sandies Creek. In 1936 a receding flood in the area exposed a small, iron cannon of the general type in use during the 1830s. However, the cannon discovered was made of iron, not bronze, and was of a much smaller caliber than a six-pound cannon. This iron cannon with a single muzzle band, without trunnions and with an oversized cascabel is believed by many to be the original "Come and Take It" cannon and is displayed at the Gonzales Memorial Museum and occasionally elsewhere within Texas. This cannon closely conforms to the picture of the cannon drawn by Sarah DeWitt on the original "Come and Take It" flag, having a repair near on the once-spiked touch hole and a heavy, protruding cascabel or butt. The inside muzzle diameter is a mere 1.20 inches, allowing it to accommodate a ball of only 30 millimeters.

Version 2. The Gonzales cannon successfully made the journey to the Alamo and was utilized there as one of the twenty-one cannon defending the Alamo during Santa Anna's March 6 assault. Following the fall of the Alamo, the Mexican army melted down the Gonzales cannon, along with the many others captured there.

Is the small bore cannon on display in the Gonzales Memorial Museum actually the "Come and Take It" cannon or was the cannon melted down by the Mexican army after the battle of the Alamo?

THE ALAMO'S EIGHTEEN-POUNDER

This large, probably iron cannon was landed in Texas at the port of Velasco with the volunteer company of New Orleans Greys arriving aboard the schooner Columbus.

By December 1835 the cannon had been laboriously transported to the Alamo where it was mounted on the southwest corner of the old mission. Since it was the Alamo's heaviest armament it was carefully sited by the mission's interim commander, Lieutenant Colonel James C. Neill, and his engineer, Green B. Jameson.

Among the soldiers servicing the eighteen-pounder was Tejano Damacio Ximenes who had previously fought under Travis at the first insurgent victory routing the occupying Mexican garrison at Anahuac.

The eighteen-pounder was fired in response to Santa Anna's demand for Travis' unconditional surrender of the Alamo. Private Ximenes probably was among the crewmen firing that shot from their position on the southwest corner of the Alamo

Ximenes, among many others, was killed during the successful Mexican assault during which the eighteen-pounder was turned about to blast the flood of Mexican soldiers climbing over the northern wall and threatening the Alamo from within. It is believed that the eighteen-pounder was eventually melted down, as the Gonzales cannon may have been, by the Mexican army to prevent its use were it recaptured.

THE "TWIN SISTERS" CANNON

During the Texas Revolution, many sympathizers with the Texas cause donated provisions, equipment and funds to Texas. Among them were the citizens of Cincinnati, Ohio who generously had two cannon manufactured by Greenwood's Eagle Ironworks of Cincinnati and shipped to Texas via New Orleans. The manufacturer's name was etched on the butt of each cannon. Another etching near each cannon's touch hole identified it as a gift from Cincinnati.

The cannon arrived at Galveston in early April 1836 aboard the schooner *Pennsylvania*. Twin daughters, Eleanor and Elizabeth ceremoniously presented the pair of cannon to the people of Texas. Eleanor and Elizabeth were daughters of Doctor Charles Rice, all of whom arrived aboard the schooner. The coincidence of the twin daughters presenting the two cannon resulted in the nickname "Twin Sisters."

Version 1. One story, unlikely because of its dates, is that the Twin Sisters cannon were aboard the schooner *Flash* April 18-19 when Texas President David G. Burnet, Vice President Lorenzo de Zavala, and their cabinet were almost captured near Morgan's Point by Mexican cavalry commanded by Colonel Juan N. Almonte. If true, the cannon reached Galveston island along with President Burnet and his cabinet.

Version 2. The bronze nine-pounders arrived at the Texas army camp at Groce's plantation on the Brazos River on April 11, 1836. They constituted General Houston's entire artillery at the battle of San Jacinto where his small army surprised and defeated Santa Anna's larger force on April 21, 1836.

Doctor S.O. Young of Houston remembered the Twin Sisters nine-pound bronze cannon decorating the city's Market Square during his youth. He said the cannon barrels were engraved above their touch holes with the phrase "Presented to the Republic of Texas by the Ladies of Cincinnati."

At that time the town of Houston was the capital of Texas and the cannon were occasionally fired during celebrations such as Sam Houston's inauguration as President of Texas on December 13, 1841.

When Texas was admitted to the United States, the Twin Sisters were reportedly shipped to the Federal arsenal at Baton Rouge, Louisiana. In 1861 the Louisiana legislature generously donated a pair of similar cannon marked "Twin Sisters" on their carriages to Texas.

Version 3. The cannon presented to the State of Texas by Louisiana were used in the recapture of Galveston island from Federal forces in January 1863. This version of the whereabouts of the Twin Sisters maintains that Confederate veterans buried the cannon in Houston, Harrisburg or in the nearby Gulf of Mexico in August 1865 to prevent the cannons' seizure by the Federals. Although presumed burial sites have been explored extensively, the cannon have never been found.

Were these famous cannon eventually located their identity might be verified by the etchings on the touch holes and butt (if they are the original cannon) or the absence of such markings (if they are the gift twin cannons from the State of Louisiana).

SANTA ANNA'S "GOLDEN STANDARD" CANNON

Even the caliber of this, Santa Anna's only cannon at the Battle of San Jacinto, remains in dispute. Mexican Lieutenant Colonel Jose de la Pena described this cannon as a six-pounder, as did Mexican General Filisola. Sam Houston reported it as a reinforced twelve-pounder while Texas Secretary of War, General Thomas Jefferson Rusk, claimed it was a nine-pounder. Said to be made of brass, its shininess may have made it look golden, hence its name the "Golden Standard."

In any case the Golden Standard was fired at the surging Texas line three times during the battle of San Jacinto and was loaded for a fourth round before being damaged by hits from Houston's Twin Sisters cannon and overrun by the charging, screaming Texians.

Version 1. One story of the Golden Standard's after-the-battle-location is that a "nine-pound long brass pivot gun" was placed aboard the Texas warship *Independence.* This was the Texas Navy ship returning the Texas Minister to the U.S., William H. Wharton, to Texas from New Orleans on April 10, 1837. Wharton had just completed his mission, culminating in the U.S. recognition of the Republic of Texas.

But the *Independence,* nearing the Texas coast, was sighted and pursued by two better-armed Mexican warships, the *Vencedor del Alamo* and the *Libertador.* After a running gun battle and chase lasting four hours, the battered Texas schooner lowered its colors near the mouth of the Brazos River. It was the only Texas warship to surrender or to be captured in battle.

The Mexicans were jubilant. Not only had they captured an important Texas diplomat they also discovered a nine-pound pivot gun, believed to be the Golden Standard, captured by the Houston's army at San Jacinto. With much pomp and ceremony, the cannon was returned to the Mexican Navy's homeport of Vera Cruz where a celebratory welcome awaited. Despite his diplomatic status, Wharton was imprisoned in Matamoros but eventually escaped.

Version 2. Another story concerning the fate of the Golden Standard also involves the Texas Navy. After the victory at *San Jacinto* where the cannon was captured, a "nine-pound long pivot gun" was placed aboard the Republic of Texas warship coincidentally named the *San Jacinto*. During a severe storm in the Arca Islands in the Gulf of Mexico the *San Jacinto* was severely damaged and sinking but its crew and armaments, including the long brass pivot cannon, were brought aboard its sister warship *San Bernard*.

The *San Bernard* was beached at Galveston, homeport of the Texas Navy, in September 1842. After sale to a local merchant, the schooner was repaired and sold to the U.S. Navy in May 1846. Again the once-proud Texas warship was sold, this time by the U.S. Navy at auction in November 1846. The eventual fate of the Golden Standard, if still aboard the Texas Navy ship *San Bernard,* is unknown.

Or is the Golden Standard cannon on display somewhere in a Mexican naval museum?

APPENDIX H
WHAT TEXAS HISTORY TEXTS SAY ABOUT TEJANO PARTICIPATION IN THE TEXAS REVOLUTION

"The average writer of Texas history has to some extent done an injustice to the heroes of Texas by almost completely ignoring the Tejanos. The Latin-Texans were not only comrades in arms, but also part of an oppressed people who had thrown their fortunes, lives and lot in life into one common cause, the cause of independence."
Ruben Rendon Lozano, author of Viva Tejas.

A textbook* currently used in Texas public school covers the revolution in some fifty pages, primarily in two chapters. The chapters are well organized and profusely illustrated, appealing to their seventh grade audiences. There are ten individual photos or drawings of famous Texans. Two of the ten are of Sam Houston. Only one of the ten is of a Tejano, Jose Antonio Navarro.

The chapters' general thrust is an appraisal of the efforts of Texas colonists and volunteers to defeat ther Mexican armies of General-in-Chief and President of Mexico Antonio Lopez de Santa Anna. Although the Tejano contributions are acknowledged, they are almost anecdotal.

Martin de Leon is acknowledged as a colonizer and the only Mexican empresario of Tejas. He settled his colony along the Guadalupe River and established the town of Guadalupe Victoria, present day Victoria, Texas. Martin de Leon died of the chorea epidemic of 1833 but his son, Fernando, continued his ambitious work. By 1835, 162 families lived in the de Leon colony.

The text defines Tejanos as people of Mexican ancestry living in Texas. Ethnicity is also used to describe Texas "rebels" as "Most (but not all) of the rebels were Anglos."

Juan Seguin's opposition to Santa Anna's centralist policies and actions is mentioned, as is that of Placido Bennavides who also joined the revolt against Santa Anna.

Benavides' leadership at Victoria, where a number of residents opposed surrendering their cannon to Mexican General Perfecto de Cos, is mentioned. Not mentioned is Benavide's refusal to surrender his friend, relative and fellow libertarian Mariano Carbajal to the Mexican authorities seeking his arrest.

Tejano participation in the Battle of Concepcion, October 28, 1835, and the Zacate or Grass Fight on November 26 is overlooked. Concerning the siege and successful December 5-10 assault on superior Mexican forces occupying Bexar (San Antonio) Tejanos are mentioned later at the Alamo.

Many Tejanos remained loyal to Mexico, the text notes, and that "loyal" Tejanos told Santa Anna that the Alamo defenders had few supplies and provisions.

A separate box highlights Juan Seguin and the Tejanos who fought at the Alamo. Those listed as Alamo casualties are Juan Abamillo, Juan Antonio Badillo, Carlos Espalier, Gregorio Esparza, Brigido Guerrero, Damacio Jimenez (Ximenez), Toribio Losoya and Andres Nava.

Unacknowledged is Tejano Galba Fuqua of the "Gonzales Thirty-two" who died defending the Alamo. Also not mentioned is Tejano Antonio Fuentes who died during the March 6 assault.

Brigido Guerrero convinced his Mexican captors in the Alamo that he had been a prisoner of the Texans and was allowed to walk away. Nor did Toribio Losoya die in the Alamo as the text indicates.

Special mention is made of Gregorio Esparza who died in the Alamo next to the small cannon he was manning. Esparza's wife, Ana, and son Enrique--who vividly remembered the assault and burning of the defenders' bodies--were among the few within the Alamo to survive that terrible day.

"The Angel of Goliad," Panchita Alavez, receives earned accolades for her bravery and compassion for the many captured volunteers whose lives she saved in and around Goliad.

Other than the photograph of Jose Antonio Navarro, there is no mention that the Texas Declaration of Independence was signed by three Tejanos: Navarro, Ruiz and Zavala. The latter, Lorenzo de Zavala, is acknowledged as having been elected the first Vice President of the Republic of Texas.

Although some participation is mentioned, more recognition is due those Tejanos and Tejanas who richly contributed toward Texas liberty and independence.

* Lone Star, the Story of Texas, Prentice-Hall, 2003.

NOTES, REFERENCES AND SUGGESTED READING

CHAPTER ONE: EARLY YEARS

1. Guerra, Mary Ann "Chronology: The Road to Revolution" unnumbered pg following Lozano's "Viva Tejas."
2. Kingston, Mike, "A Concise History of Texas", pp.17-45.
3. Perrigo, Lynn I., "Texas and Our Spanish Southwest", pp.97-107.
4. Sons of DeWitt Colony Texas Online, "Gutierrez de Lara, Mexican-Texan: The Story of a Creole Hero", Chapter X.
5. Wikipedia Online, "Jose Francisco Ruiz", p.1.
6. De la Teja, Jesus F. "A Revolution Remembered," p.8
7. Handbook of Texas Online, "Martin de Leon", p 2.
8. Sons of DeWitt Colony Texas Online, "The DeLeon Colony" p.2.
9. Sons of DeWitt Colony Texas Online, "The Constitution of the Mexican United States", pp.2–3.
10. Perrigo. p.122.
11. Cantwell, Greg, "Stephen F. Austin, Empresario of Texas," p.161.
12. Perrigo. p.125.

CHAPTER TWO: DISCONTENT INCREASES

1. Coalson, George O., "Texas Mexicans in the Texas Revolution," p.164.
2. Kingston, Mike, "A Concise History of Texas," p.47.
3. Perrigo, Lynn I., "Texas and Our Spanish Southwest," p.108.
4. Kokernot, D.L., "The Battle of Anahuac," p.275.

5. House, Boyce, "An Incident at Velasco, 1832," p.94.
6. Lozano, Ruben R. "Viva Tejas," Introduction, unnumbered page.
7. Cantrell, Greg, "Stephen F. Austin, Empresario of Texas," p.271.
8. Guerra, Mary Ann, "Chronology: The Road to Revolution," unnumbered page following Lozano's "Viva Tejas"
9. Cleaves, W.S., "Lorenzo De Zavala in Texas," p.35.
10. Santa Anna, Antonio L., "The Mexican Side of the Texas Revolution," p.17.

CHAPTER THREE: "COME AND TAKE IT"

1. Cleaves,W.S., "Lorenzo De Zavala in Texas," p.36.
2. Sons of DeWitt Colony Texas, "Battle of Gonzales," p.3
3. Ibid. p.5.
4. De la Teja,Jesus F., "A Revolution Remembered," p.24.
5. Wikipedia, "Salvador Flores," p.2.
6. Handbook of Texas Online, "DeLeon, Martin" p.2.
7. Acosta, Teresa and Winegarten, Ruthe, "Las Tejadas," pp. 41-42.

CHAPTER FOUR: RETAKING GOLIAD AND SAN ANTONIO DE BEXAR

1. Coalson, George O. "Texas Mexicans in the Texas Revolution," p.167
2. Hardin, Stephen L., "Texian Iliad," p.29.
3. Handbook of Texas Online, "Benavides, Placido", p.1.
4. De la Teja, Jesus F. "A Revolution Remembered," p.77.
5. Wikipedia, "Salvador Flores," p.2.
6. Stout, Jay A. "Slaughter at Goliad," p. 36.
7. Field, Joseph E., "Three Years in Texas," pp.15-16.
8. Wikipedia. p.2.
9. Coalson,George O., p.170.
10. Field, Joseph E. p.20.
11. Acosta, Teresa and Winegarten, Ruthe, "Las Tejanas," p.39.
12. Lindley, Thomas R., "Alamo Traces," p.262.
13. Lord, Walter, "A Time to Stand," p.57.
14. De la Pena, Jose E., "With Santa Anna in Texas," p.14.

CHAPTER FIVE: TENSIONS AT GOLIAD AND MASSING OF TROOPS AT THE ALAMO

1. Coalson, George O., "Texas Mexicans in the Texas Revolution," p.172.
2. De la Teja, Jesus F., "A Revolution Remembered," p.79.
3. Becerra, Francisco, "A Mexican Sergeant's Recollections of the Alamo and San Jacinto," pp.25-27.
4. Miller, Thomas L., "Mexican-Texans at the Alamo," p.36.
5. De la Pena, Jose Enrique, "With Santa Anna in Texas," pp.44-45
6. Ibid.

CHAPTER SIX: THE ASSAULT AND AFTERMATH

1. Becerra, Francisco, "A Mexican Sergeant's Recollections of the Alamo and San Jacinto," p.6.
2. Ibid., pp.20-24.
3. Lord, Walter, "A Time to Stand," pp.155-156.
4. Becerra, pp.24-25.
5. Lord, Walter, p.208.
6. Becerra, pp.24-25.
7. Hardin, Stephen L., "Texian Iliad," p.155.
8. Lord, pp.209-210.
9. Ibid.

CHAPTER SEVEN: TEJANO CASUALTIES AT THE ALAMO

1. Miller, Thomas L. "Mexican-Texans at the Alamo," p. 33.
2. Lord, Walter, "A Time to Stand," pp.214-219.
3. Miller, Thomas L., pp.35-40.

CHAPTER EIGHT: GENERAL URREA'S SUCCESFUL SKIRMISHES AND THE CONVENTION MEETING AT WASHINGTON-ON-THE-BRAZOS

1. Fuller, R.M., "The Fall of the Alamo," p.4.
2. Santa Anna, Martinez Caro, Filisola, Urrea and Tornel, "The Mexican Side of the Texas Revolution," pp 215-216.
3. De la Pena, Jose Enrique, "With Santa Anna in Texas," p.68.
4. Ibid., p.84.
5. Ibid., p.68.
6. Santa Anna, Martinez Caro, Filisola, Urrea and Tornel, p. 217.
7. Lord, Walter, "A Time to Stand," p.211.
8. De la Pena, p.4.

CHAPTER NINE: EYES ON GOLIAD

1. Field, Joseph E., "Three Years in Texas," p.29.
2. Sons of DeWitt Colony Texas, "Men of San Patricio, Refugio and Goliad, Spring 1836." pp.3-4.
3. Ibid. pp 4-5.
4. Nofi, Albert A. "The Alamo and the Texas War for Independence," p.140.
5. De la Pena, Jose Enrique, "With Santa Anna in Texas," pp.70-71.
6. Hardin, Stephen L. "Texian Iliad," p.165.
7. Stout, Jay A. "Slaughter at Goliad," p. 27.
8. Ibid, p. 77.
9. Sons of DeWitt Colony Texas, "Men of San Patricio, Refugio and Goliad, Spring, 1836," pp. 5-12.
10. Field, Joseph E. pp.50-51.
11. Hardin, Stephen L., "Texian Iliad," pp.171-172.
12. Santa Anna, Martinez Caro, Filisola, Urrea and Tornel, "The Mexican Side of the Texas Revolution," p.220.Filisola, Urrea and Tornel, "The Mexican Side of the Texas Revolution," p.228.
13. Hardin, Stephen L., p.173.
14. Santa Anna, Martinez Caro, Filisola, Urrea and Tornel, p.236.
15. Ibid., p.18.
16. Stout, Jay A., p.205.

CHAPTER TEN: HOUSTON'S RETREAT

1. Hardin, Stephen L. "Texian Iliad," p.180.
2. Santa Anna, Martinez Caro, Filisola, Urrea and Tornel, "The Mexican Side of the Texas Revolution," p.31.
3. Hardin, Stephen L., p.181.
4. Moore, Stephen L., "Eighteen Minutes," p. 112.
5. Hardin, p.183.
6. Ibid., p.186.
7. Ibid., p.189.
8. Moore, Stephen L. "Eighteen Minutes," p.247.
9. Seguin, Juan N., "A Revolution Remembered," pp.108-109.
10. Ibid.
11. Becerra, Francisco, "A Mexican Sergeant's Recollections of the Alamo and San Jacinto," p.44.

CHAPTER ELEVEN: "WILL YOU COME TO THE BOWER I HAVE SHADED FOR YOU?"

1. Nofi, Albert A. "The Alamo and the Texas War for Independence," p.152.
2. Seguin, Juan N., "A Revolution Remembered," p.83.
3. Tolbert, Frank X., "The Day of San Jacinto," p.135.
4. Seguin, Juan N., p.83.
5. MacDonald, L. Lloyd, "Tejanos in the 1835 Texas Revolution," pp. 274-275.
6. Nofi, Albert A., p.157.
7. Lord, Walter, "A Time to Stand," p.196.
8. Santa Anna, Martinez Caro, Filisola, Urrea and Tornel, "The Mexican Side of the Texas Revolution," p.24.
9. Ibid., p.31.
10. De la Pena, Jose Enrique, "With Santa Anna in Texas," p. 127.

CHAPTER TWELVE: FRIEND, NOW FOE?

1.   Nance, Joseph M., "After San Jacinto," pp.46-47.
2.   Seguin, Juan N., "A Revolution Remembered," p.174.
3.   Ibid. p.97.
6.   Ibid.
5. Ibid.

BIBLIOGRAPHY

BOOKS

Acosta, Teresa, and Winegarten, Ruthie. Las Tejanas. Austin, Texas: University of Texas Press, 2003.

Alonzo, Armando C. Tejano Legacy. Albuqueque, New Mexico: University of New Mexico Press, 1998.

Barker, Eugene C. Life of Stephen F. Austin, Father of Texas. Austin, Texas: Texas State Historical Association, 1949.

Becerra, Francisco. A Mexican Sergeant's Recollection of the Alamo and San Jacinto. Austin, Texas: Jenkins Publishing Company, 1980.

Bradfield, Jane. RX: Take One Cannon. Fort Collins, Colorado: Old Army Press, 1981.

Brown, Gary. John Walker Fannin. Plano, Texas: Republic of Texas Press, 2000.

Cantrell, Gregg. Stephen F. Austin, Empresario of Texas. New Haven, Connecticut: Yale University Press, 1999.

Coalson, George O. Texas Mexicans in the Texas Revolution. From Colony to Republic: Readings in American History to 1877. Houston, Texas: Cayo del Grullo Press, 1983.

Davis, Joe Tom. Legendary Texans. Austin, Texas: Eakin Press, 1982-86.

De la Pena, Jose Enrique. With Santa Anna in Texas. College Station, Texas: Texas A&M University Press, 1975.

De la Teja, Jesus F. A Revolution Remembered. Austin, Texas: State House Press, 1991.

De La Teja, Jesus F. Tejano Leadership in Mexican and Revolutionary Texas.College Station, Texas: Texas A&M University Press, 2010.

Fehrenbach, T.R., Siegel, Stanley, Crowley, David and Viola, H. Lone Star: A History of Texas and the Texans. New York, New York: American Legacy Press, 1983.

Fehrenbach, T.R., Siegel, Stanley, Crowley, David and Viola, H. Lone Star, the Story of Texas. Upper Saddle River, N.J.: Prentice-Hall, 2003.

Fields, Joseph E. Three Years in Texas. Austin, Texas: The Steck Company, 1935.

Filisola, Vicente. The History of the War in Texas. Austin, Texas: The Eakin Press, 1985.

Fuller, R.M. The Fall of the Alamo. Bryan, Texas: Fuller Printing Company, 1979.

Hardin, Stephen L. Texian Iliad. Austin, Texas: University of Texas Press, 1994.

Kingston, Mike. A Concise History of Texas. Houston, Texas: Gulf Publishing Company, 1988.

Lindley, Thomas R. Alamo Traces. Lanham, New York: Republic of Texas Press, 2003.

Linn, John J. Reminiscences of Fifty Years in Texas. New York: D. and J. Sadlier Co., 1883.

Lord, Walter. A Time to Stand. Lincoln, Nebraska: University of Nebraska Press, 1961.

Lozano, Ruben Rendon. Viva Tejas. San Antonio, Texas: The Alamo Press, 1936.

Maberry, Robert. Texas Flags. College Station, Texas: Texas A&M University Press, 2001.

MacDonald, L. Lloyd. Tejanos in the 1835 Texas Revolution. Gretna, Louisiana: Pelican Publishing Company, 2009.

Matovina, Timothy M. The Alamo Remembered: Tejano Accounts and Perspectives. Austin, Texas: University of Texas Press, 1995.

Montejano, David. Anglos and Mexicans in the Making of Texas. Austin, Texas: University of Texas Press, 1987.

Moore, Stephen L. Eighteen Minutes. Lanham, Maryland: Republic of Texas Press, 2004.

Nance, Joseph M. After San Jacinto. Austin, Texas: University of Texas Press, 1963.

Navarro, Jose Antonio. Defending Mexican Valor in Texas.Abilene, Texas: State House Press, 1995.

Nofi, Albert A. The Alamo and the Texas War for Independence. New York, New York: Da Capo Press, 1994.

Perrigo, Lynn I. Texas and Our Spanish Southwest. Dallas, Texas: Banks Upshaw and Company, 1960.

Santa Anna, Antonio Lopez de. The Eagle. Austin, Texas: Pemberton Press, 1967.

Santa Anna, Antonio Lopez de, Martinez Caro, Filisola, Urrea and Tornel. The Mexican Side of the Texas Revolution. Washington, D.C.: Documentary Publications, 1971.

Stout, Jay A. Slaughter at Goliad. Annapolis, Maryland: Naval Institute Press, 2008.

Tolbert, Frank X. The Day of San Jacinto. New York, New York: McGraw-Hill, 1959.

Walraven, Bill and Marjorie K. The Magnificent Barbarians. Austin, Texas: The Eakin Press, 1993.

LETTERS AND REPORTS

Morgan to J. Reed, May 11, 1843. Morgan Papers. Rosenberg Library, Galveston, Texas.

Letters, The Austin Papers. ed. Eugene C. Barker. Austin, Texas: American Historical Association, 1923.

Orders, Santa Anna to Ramirez y Sesma, December 7, 1835. Referentes a la Campagna Sobre las Colonias Sublevadas de Tejas, verificado el ano 1836. Numero novena.

The Handbook of Victoria County. Austin: Texas State Historical Association, 1990.

ON-LINE RESOURCES

Early Texas History:
   The Hunt for the Cincinnati Twin Sister Cannon

Fuqua-Family
   The Fuquas

Handbook of Texas:
  Aldrete, Jose Miguel
  Battle of Refugio
  Benavides, Placido
  De Leon, Martin
  Espalier, Carlos
  Herrera, Blas Maria
  Twin Sisters

Sons of DeWitt Colony Texas:
  Articles of Agreement at San Jacinto
  Battle of Gonzales
  Goliad Region January-27 March 1836
  Gutierrez de Lara,Mexican-Texan: The Story of a Creole Hero
   Hispanic Texian Patriots in the Struggle for Independence
  Martin de Leon
  Old Gonzalez Eighteen
  Procedures of the Gonzales Ayuntamiento 1835-1836
  The Hispanic Experience-Tejanos in the Texas Revolution

TAMU Education:
  The Alamo Cannon

Texas State Library:
  Jose Antonio Navarro
  Lorenzo de Zavala

Wikipedia:
  Battle of the Brazos River
  Battle of Concepcion
  Manuel N. Flores
  Salvador Flores
  Francisco Ruiz
  List of Alamo Defenders
  List of Texas Revolution Battles

The Alamo Central Forum

Roots Web Texas Revolution:
  The Golden Standard

PERIODICALS

Cleaves, W.S. Lorenzo de Zavala in Texas. Southwestern Historical Quarterly Vol 36, July 1932. Austin Texas: Texas Historical Society.
De Leon, Arnoldo, Tejanos and the Texas War for Independence. Albuqueque, New Mexico: New Mexico Historical Review, April, 1986.
Estep, Raymond. Lorenzo de Zavala and the Texas Revolution. Austin, Texas: Southwestern Historical Quarterly 57, January, 1954. Austin, Texas: Texas Historical Society.
Gonzales Inquirer Special Supplement, September 30-October 2, 2011. "Come and Take It." Gonzales, Texas.
House, Bryce. An Incident at Velasco, 1832. Austin, Texas: Southwestern Historical Quarterly, LXIV, 1960.
Kokernot, D.L. The Battle of Anahuac. Austin, Texas: Southwestern Historical Quarterly, XLII, 1939.
Miller, Thomas L. Mexican-Texans at the Alamo. Journal of Mexican American History, 2, Fall, 1971. Santa Barbara, California: A. Cortez.
Spellman, Paul N. Santa Anna's Revived Invasion Plans Crushed at Salado Creek. San Antonio, Texas: San Antonio Express News, September 13, 1992.
Telegraph and Texas Register. Houston, Texas, November 26, 1836.